THE FACE OF IMPERIALISM

THE FACE OF
IMPERIALISM

MICHAEL PARENTI

Paradigm Publishers
Boulder • London

Copyright © 2011 Paradigm Publishers

Published in the United States by Paradigm Publishers, 2845 Wilderness Place, Boulder, CO 80301 USA.

Paradigm Publishers is the trade name of Birkenkamp & Company, LLC, Dean Birkenkamp, President and Publisher.

Library of Congress Cataloging-in-Publication Data

Parenti, Michael, 1933–
  The face of imperialism / Michael Parenti.
     p. cm.
  Includes bibliographical references and index.
  ISBN 978-1-59451-917-8 (hardcover : alk. paper) — ISBN 978-1-59451-918-5 (pbk. : alk. paper)
  1. Imperialism. 2. United States—Foreign relations—1989– I. Title.
  JC359.P34 2011
  325'.320973—dc22

                                                                    2010047856

Printed and bound in the United States of America on acid-free paper that meets the standards of the American National Standard for Permanence of Paper for Printed Library Materials.

Designed and Typeset by Straight Creek Bookmakers.

14 13 12 11 1 2 3 4 5

But who can live for long
In an euphoric dream;
Out of the mirror they stare,
Imperialism's face
And the international wrong.

—W. H. Auden

Contents

1

Thinking About Empire

IN THIS AGE OF EMPIRE, how do we arrive at the truth? Many of our political perceptions are shaped by culturally prefigured templates implanted in our minds without our conscious awareness. To become critically aware of these ingrained opinions and images is not only an act of self-education; it is an act of self-defense. This seems especially true when dealing with matters of global impact, such as the nature of empire.

Orthodoxy as "Objectivity"

In 1932, Carl Becker was among the first to give currency to the phrase *the climate of opinion*. Becker argued that ideas and notions about reality do not spring forth from the mind in a social vacuum. They are pursued because they seem to fit into the ongoing climate of opinion.[1]

They reinforce each other, gaining acceptance through circulation and repetition. The notions that fit into the prevailing climate of opinion are more likely to be accepted as objective, while those that clash with it are usually seen as beyond the pale and lacking in credibility. So, more often than we realize, we accept or decline an idea, depending on its acceptability within the ongoing opinion climate.

In other words, the mental selectors we use to organize our perceptions are *not* mostly of our own creation. Much about our personal perception is not all that personal; rather, it is shaped by a variety of forces and conditions outside ourselves, such as the dominant ideology (or "dominant paradigm"), the conventional social values, one's position in the social structure, the available flow of information and disinformation, and the potential benefits and losses attached to the perceptions and pronouncements one makes. On that last point it is obbligato to reference Upton Sinclair's remark: "It is difficult to get a man to understand something, when his salary depends upon his not understanding it."[2]

If what we call "objectivity" is really little more than a conformity of mainstream bias, then isn't one paradigm about as reliable—or unreliable—as another? Is all truth, then, nothing more than opinion and belief? If not, what makes a heterodox analysis better than an orthodox one?

First, radical views that are outside the mainstream generally (but not always) are more reliable than the dominant view because they are more regularly challenged and tested against evidence. They do not get to float freely down the mainstream. They cannot rest on the orthodox power to foreclose dissent, and they are not supported by the unanimity of bias that passes for objectivity.

Second, we can value an opinion by the function(s) it serves. The *heterodox* view has a special task: to contest the prevailing orthodoxy, to broaden the boundaries of debate, to wake people up, to unearth suppressed data. The function of orthodox or conventional opinion is just the opposite: to keep the parameters of discourse as narrow as possible, to dismiss evidence that ill fits the dominant paradigm. Hence, all opinions are not of the same value. It depends on what they are being used for, what interests they serve.

We have all observed that if something does not fit what people believe, they marshal their reserve defenses. Rarely when faced with contrary evidence do they discard their preciously held beliefs. And if they cannot challenge the validity of what confronts them, they have *fallback positions* that explain to their satisfaction the data that do not fit the pictures in their heads.

When the orthodox view becomes so entrenched, evidence becomes irrelevant.

Broaching certain subjects casts doubt on the credibility and sanity of the dissident who dares to raise a question. Consider such inflammatory topics as: the legitimacy of the 2004 presidential election in the United States, the Shangri-La image of Tibet before the Chinese invasion, the findings of the Warren Commission regarding the assassination of President John Kennedy, the number of people killed by this or that tyrant, the Clinton/NATO/CIA war against Yugoslavia, the unanswered questions of the 9/11 Commission, a class power analysis of the American political system, and the absence of political-economic content in public policy debates.

Such topics raise issues that cross *the boundary of allowable opinion*. They move into forbidden terrain and are therefore dismissed out of hand, denied the opportunity for rational discourse. Through a process of immediate assertion and intensive repetition, the universe of discourse is preempted and monopolized. This is one way the dominant paradigm is maintained. One crosses the lines beyond permissible opinion only at a risk to one's intellectual reputation or even one's career.

The Myth of Innocent Empires

The presence of self-legitimating ideological boundaries is evident in the discussion about empire. When writing a book about ancient Rome, I discovered that much of the historic literature on empire is rather favorable.[3] Empires have been hailed as grand accomplishments, bringing stability and peace where before there had been only squabbling tribes. We even give empires laudatory peace names, such as Pax Romana and Pax Britannica.

Empires also are sometimes seen as innocent unintentional accretions that arise stochastically—that is, by chance, without benefit of any kind of "conspiratorial" planning or even consistent causality. Years ago we used to hear that the British Empire was put together in a "fit of absentmindedness." More recently, four months after the United States invaded Iraq, and referring to that event, *The Economist*, a conservative British publication, wrote, "Empires are born in funny ways, and sometimes via the law of unintended consequences by accident."[4]

In fact, empires are not innocent, absent-minded, accidental accretions. They are given purposive direction by rulers who consciously mobilize vast amounts of personnel and materials in order to plunder other lands and peoples. The British, for instance, did not just happen to find themselves in India. They pushed their way in with all deliberate force and rapacious intent. The Americans did not just mistakenly stumble into Iraq because of some misinformation that the Iraqis were linked to Al Qaeda and possessed weapons of mass destruction. The White House coterie that pursued war had been calling for intervention against Iraq for at least a year *before* the 2001 attack on the World Trade Center, and well before there was ever any thought of Al Qaeda terrorist networks in Baghdad or Iraqi weapons of mass destruction.[5]

Despite the sympathetic treatment accorded empires by numerous historians and others, the term *empire* was not comfortably applied to the United States during most of the twentieth century, at least not by us Americans. Other countries had colonies, but America had "territories" and "possessions"—so I was taught in grade school. The word *empire* remained suspect, an unbecoming appellation that besmirched our shining republic.

No wonder that when I wrote my book *Against Empire* in 1995, some of my American compatriots thought it was wrong of me to call the United States an empire. It was widely believed that US rulers did not pursue empire; they intervened abroad only out of self-defense or for humanitarian rescue operations or to restore order in a troubled region or overthrow tyranny and propagate democracy. But some few years later, oddly enough everyone started talking about the United States as an empire and writing books with titles like *Sorrows of Empire, Follies of Empire, Twilight of Empire, Empire of Illusion*—all referring to the United States.

One professor, writing in *Harvard Magazine,* was unequivocal about his country's *force majeure* role in the world: "We are militarily dominant around the world.... A political unit that has overwhelming superiority of military power, and uses that power to influence the behavior of other states is called an empire.... [O]ur goal is not combating a rival but maintaining our [supreme] imperial position and maintaining imperial order."[6]

One also could hear right-wing pundits announcing on television that we are an empire, with all the responsibilities and opportunities of empire, and as the strongest nation in the world we have every right to act as such—as if having the power gives US leaders an inherent entitlement to exercise it upon others as they see fit. So liberals and conservatives began to lay claim to the notion of empire and treat it as worthy of public embrace.

What is going on here? I asked myself at the time. How is it that after years of denial and denunciation, many individuals now feel free to talk about empire when they mean *American* empire? The answer, I realized, is that the word has been divested of its full meaning. "Empire" seems to mean simply *dominion* and *power*, most notably *military* power. Thus Chalmers Johnson tells us that the United States has an empire of bases rather than colonies. He sees a US government that is "obsessed" with maintaining military dominance over the entire world. The 730 or more US military bases that ring the globe, he claims, are proof that the "United States prefers to deal with other nations through the use or threat of force rather than negotiations, commerce, or cultural interaction." (In fact, the United States constantly uses negotiations, commerce, and cultural interaction along with a whole arsenal of other modes of influence.) The rise of American militarism, Johnson goes on to say, is accompanied by layers of bureaucracy and secrecy designed to circumvent public scrutiny and keep power in the hands of the Pentagon.[7]

What is missing from these kinds of analyses and even more so from the public discourse in general is the *political-economic content* of empire. In other words, while we hear a lot about empire and militarism, we hear very little about *imperialism*. This is strange, for imperialism is what empires do. Imperialism is the very activity of empire. (Another name for empire is *imperium*.)

By *imperialism* I do not mean just power and dominion; I mean the process of transnational investment and capital accumulation. Nor would I pretend to be the only investigator who thinks of imperialism that way. There are a number of advanced scholars—such as James Petras, Eva Golinger, Gregory Elich, Gerald Horne, Henry Veltmeyer, Francis Shor, and David Harvey—who offer a more developed and accurate view of the forces of imperialism.[8]

For latter-day liberal converts like Chalmers Johnson, however, the word *imperialism* is used in the same empty way as is the word *empire:* to denote dominion and control with little attention given to the powerful economic interests that operate as a motor force behind US policy. Johnson and a host of others have produced shallow critiques of empire, characterizing US interventionist policies as "reckless," "misguided," "inept," "bumbling," "insensitive," "overreaching," "self-deceptive," "deluded," "driven by false assumptions," and "presuming a mandate from God," while ladened with "tragic mistakes" and "imperial hubris."[9] They see all this as a mindless proclivity embedded in the American psyche or culture. We are left to conclude that US leaders are chronically deluded, stupid, and incapable of learning from past experience; they lack the splendid intelligence of their liberal critics. For the critics, empire has little to do with economic class interests and is mostly a product of an aggrandizing national temperament incited by myopic overweening leaders.

Not Just "Power for Power's Sake"

In this book, *imperialism* is defined as follows: the process whereby the dominant investor interests in one country bring to bear military and financial power upon another country in order to expropriate the land, labor, capital, natural resources, commerce, and markets of that other country. In short, empires do not just pursue power for power's sake. There are real material interests at stake, fortunes to be made many times over. Behind Colonel Blimp there stood the East India Company and the Bank of England. Behind Teddy Roosevelt and the US Marines there stood the United Fruit Company and Wall Street. The intervention is intended to enrich the investors and keep the world safe for them.

For centuries the ruling interests in Western Europe and, later on, North America and Japan laid claim to most of planet Earth, including the labor of indigenous peoples (as workers or slaves), their incomes (through colonial taxation or debt control or other means), their markets, and the abundant treasures of their lands: their gold, silver, diamonds, slaves, copper, rum, molasses, hemp, flax, ebony, timber, sugar, fruits, tobacco, palm oil, ivory, iron, tin, nickel, coal, cotton, corn, and more recently, uranium, manganese, titanium, bauxite, oil, and—say it again—oil, and numerous other things.[10]

Empires are enormously profitable for the investor interests of the imperial nation but enormously costly to the people of the colonized country. Even today, plundered populations bemoan the *resource curse*, knowing from bitter experience that countries rich in natural resources usually end up as *losers*. Many of the countries of Africa, Asia, and Latin America are rich, only the people are poor. The imperialists search out rich places, not barren ones, to plunder.

Arid Spain and Portugal siphoned off South America's gold; tiny Holland dominated vast Indonesia. Britain, barren except for coal, built an imperial swap shop of grain, lumber, cotton, tea, tobacco, opium, gems, silver, and slaves. Japan, less than a century out of its bamboo-armor era, conquered much of China for its iron and coal. The postcolonial era [1950 to today] hasn't been any easier on the resource-rich have-nots.[11]

In addition to the pillage of their lands, the people of these targeted countries are frequently killed in large numbers by the intruders. This is another thing that empires do which too often goes unmentioned in the historical and political literature of countries like the United States, Britain, and France. Empires impoverish whole populations and slaughter huge numbers of innocent people. Along with those who are killed outright, the victims should include the many shattered survivors whose lives are reduced to a miserable subsistence or a grieving and painful undoing.[12]

The purpose of the imperial killings is to prevent alternative, independent, self-defining nations from emerging—nations that might threaten the imperium's hegemonic control, thereby jeopardizing its political-economic advantages. Just to give one example of the imperium's carnage, during the Vietnam War about a million and a half Vietnamese were killed: 185,000 South Vietnamese soldiers, 924,000 North Vietnamese and Vietcong soldiers, and 415,000 additional civilians. About 58,000 American troops also perished.[13] The great majority of these killings were perpetrated by US military forces with their vastly superior fire power.

Regarding imperialism's capacity to deliver death and destruction, consider the case of Iraq. In 1991, twelve years before Iraq was invaded and occupied by President George W. Bush, his father, President George H. W. Bush, launched an aerial war (the Gulf War) against that same nation. At that time, Iraq's standard of living was the highest in the Middle East. Iraqis enjoyed free medical care and free education. Literacy had reached about 80 percent. University students of *both genders* received scholarships to study at home and abroad. Most of the economy was state owned. Iraqi ruler Saddam Hussein was pressing for a larger portion of the international oil market. In the eyes of the Western imperialists, Saddam was charting an independent course and was guilty of committing *economic nationalism*. He would have to be taught a lesson. His country needed to be bombed back into the Third World from which it was emerging.

In the six weeks of aerial attacks in 1991, US planes (with minor assistance from other NATO powers) destroyed more than 90 percent of Iraq's electrical capacity, and much of its telecommunication systems including television and radio stations, along with its flood control, irrigation, sewage treatment, water purification, and hydro-electric systems. Domestic herds and poultry farms suffered heavy losses. US planes burned grain fields with incendiary bombs and hit hundreds of schools, hospitals, rail stations, bus stations, air raid shelters, mosques, and historic sites. Factories that produced textiles, cement, petrochemicals, and phosphate were hit repeatedly. So were the refineries, pipelines, and storage tanks of Iraq's oil industry. Some

200,000 Iraqi civilians and soldiers were killed in those six weeks. Nearly all the aerial attackers employed laser-guided depleted-uranium missiles, leaving hundreds of tons of radioactive matter spread over much of the country, leading to tens of thousands of more deaths in the following years, including many from what normally would be treatable and curable illnesses.[14] Twelve years later, Bush Jr. invaded Iraq and wreaked further death and destruction upon that country (see Chapter 9).

So, the face of imperialism reveals endless carnage. This should be kept in mind when using such neutral terms as *foreign policy, international relations, overseas commitments, régime change,* and *intervention.*

Instrumental "Truths" and the Dominant Paradigm

The imperialists are among the socio-economic and political elites who are the keepers of the *dominant paradigm.* The dominant paradigm is the prevailing ideology or mode of thought that purports to explain how and why society functions as it does. The purveyors of the dominant paradigm in the United States and the western world in general most certainly believe in it. The ideology they propagate defines their world for them. It is the magic alchemy that lends virtue to their class supremacy, assuring them of their indispensable worth to society. The dominant paradigm tells them that all their wrongfully acquired gains and privileges are rightfully theirs.

Along with one of their eighteenth-century progenitors, Alexander Hamilton, the corporate economic elites believe that the country should be run by "the rich and the wellborn." They deeply feel they are deserving of their station in life. They believe the United States should lead the world and they should lead the United States. They are convinced that the poor are the authors of their own poverty, and that the working class consists of a troublesome lot who need to be reined in along with the middle class—both of whom are admonished to ratchet down their standard of living so that those at the very top can get an ever larger portion of the pie and an ever firmer grip on the servings.

Do those who put forth the lies of empire believe what they tell us? Sometimes yes, sometimes no. That an opinion buttresses one's self-interest does not necessarily mean it is hypocritically embraced. If anything, it is all the more fervently held and is believed to be correct by the very fact that it serves one's advantage so well. Do the empire builders believe the propaganda they put out in support of specific policies? To be sure, sometimes they deliberately fabricate, as when you catch them in blatant inconsistencies. Much of the time truth is not even given consideration. It is much like the advertising world: the prime concern when selling a product is not "is it true?" but "will it sell?" Is the message effective? Is it getting across? If so, then it is "true" so to speak, and we can go with it. If not, then it is discarded. The approach to truth is purely instrumental.

Take the propaganda line that President George W. Bush used for almost a year in regard to Iraq: *stay the course.* Eventually the administration ascertained that the public did not like the idea of indefinitely staying the course in Iraq. It made them feel as if there was no hope for a change in policy, no hope for ending the war. Hence, sometime in early 2007 the White House stopped using that phrase not because they no longer believed it (assuming they ever did) but because it was not serving their propaganda goal, their big sell.

Do those who preside over the US empire believe in their own virtue? All people, parties, and national leaders believe in their own virtue. But even more so, more than anything else in the world, with the utmost dedication and ferocity, they believe in protecting and advancing their own material interests. And, as we shall see, they do whatever it takes to do so.

2

The Omnipresent Arsenal

LIKE EMPIRES BEFORE IT, the American imperium needs to muster immense quantities of military might. An empire finds its birth, growth, and perhaps even its eventual death in its *force majeure*, its irresistible armed power. Born of its own aggrandizement, an empire lives in a world of real or imagined enemies who must be subdued with force and violence.

An Expensive Parasite

The imperial nation conceives of only two kinds of nations beyond its boundaries: *satellites* (or vassal states) and *enemies* (potential and actual). Among the satellites can be included "allies," those lesser powers that remain friendly by staying more or less in line with the imperial transnational investment policies of large-scale capital accumulation. The satellite is a vassal state bonded to the imperium. Among the enemies (or "potential" enemies) is any country that seeks to chart an independent and self-defining course, to use its land, natural resources, capital, labor, and markets for its own development and possibly for regional hegemony.

Each new imperial acquisition creates a broadened perimeter, yet another area to defend against some real or imagined adversary. The empire builders know no rest. They require ever larger budgets and ever more elaborate weaponry. The corporate investors batten on defense contracts, leaving the taxpayer to bear the crushing costs.

In 2009, the Obama administration proposed a "stimulus package" to counteract the deep recession that afflicted the corporate economy. The package consisted of $787 billion in spending programs presumably designed to create jobs and stimulate growth. (Although one critic noted that the stimulus plan was "overloaded with business-friendly tax cuts and too short on labor-intensive projects to put people to work right away."[1]) Left unmentioned in the debate over the package is that the US corporate economy has been living off annual stimulus packages ever since World War II. They are called "defense expenditures." Every year the military spending package is by far the largest item in the discretionary federal budget.

As to be expected, these colossal allocations are encouraged by corporate America, first, because such expenditures create a military might that boosts corporate global hegemony; and second, because military contracts are risk-free, set without competitive bidding or adequate oversight. They come with guaranteed cost overruns and bring in superlative profits. Defense spending does not have to struggle with sluggish consumer demand; there are always more advanced weapons to develop, obsolete weaponry to replace, soldiers to feed and shelter, and new wars to be fought.

These, then, comprise the two basic reasons why the US assiduously remains an armed superpower even in the absence of a comparable opponent. First, keeping the world safe for global capital accumulation requires a massive military establishment. Second, a massive military itself constitutes a source of immense capital accumulation.

The centrists and liberals dare not challenge these military appropriations for fear of being seen as faltering in their devotion to "keep America strong." Obama's 2009 stimulus package was heavily contested because it was for civilian economic purposes rather than for empire and war—in contrast to the huge 2010 defense spending bills that Congress passed with relatively little debate.

The enormous national debt the United States carries, and the heavy tax burden the public bears in servicing that debt, is largely an outgrowth of the gargantuan sums expended on wars and military budgets, the cumulative multi-*trillion*-dollar expense of maintaining a growing global empire for the past sixty years or more.

Some reactionaries argue that the debt is caused mostly by Social Security payments and other entitlements, all of which threaten to go broke in some years ahead. In fact, over the past half century or more the Social Security Trust Fund has been self-sufficient, taking in more money than it spends. By 2010 it contained an accumulated $2.6 *trillion* surplus.[2]

Cui Bono?

Numbering among the victims of imperialism are the common people of the imperial nation itself, those who pay the costs of empire with their blood and taxes. *The empire feeds off the republic.* The populace does without essentials so that the patricians can pursue their far-off plunder. The center is bled so that the perimeter can continue to expand.

By 2011 the wars in Afghanistan and Iraq had cost over 5,000 American lives, along with tens of thousands more wounded or disabled, and hundreds of thousands of Iraqi and Afghani deaths.

Suicide rates among US veterans from these two wars remained dramatically higher than in the rest of the US population. Mental health breakdowns were now the leading cause of hospital admissions for the military, higher than physical injuries. On any given night, tens of thousands of homeless veterans were living on our nation's streets.[3]

As we moved deeper into the "Great Recession," almost every state and municipality in the United States was facing a budget crisis with serious shortfalls in revenues, record debts, and harsh cutbacks in human services. But one component of government, the Defense Department, suffered no shortage of funding. In 2010, the Pentagon and related agencies expended somewhere between $850 billion to $1 trillion, if we count the indirect costs of war and empire, such as veterans benefits and medical costs, annual debt payments due to military spending, covert military and intelligence operations, the 70 percent of federal research and development funds that goes to the military, "supplementary appropriations" for specific wars as in Iraq and Afghanistan, and defense expenses picked up by nonmilitary agencies including "defense-related activities" of the General Services Administration, along with the Energy Department's nuclear weapons programs, which consumes more than half of that department's budget.[4] This was a vastly larger sum than what all fifty states of the union together spent on education, housing, police, fire fighting, roads, hospitals, human services, occupational safety, and the like.

With only 5 percent of the world's population, the United States now accounts for almost 50 percent of the world's military spending. In second place is China, with 6.6 percent of the world's expenditure on arms. In the past decade the US allocated over $6 *trillion* on war and preparation for war.[5] Forty percent of the US military budget goes for overhead. One critic notes that the Pentagon cannot account for much of its funds, property, and supplies. "[I]t cooks its own books to make them appear in balance, and it makes new spending decisions based on the phony data." Many years of reports by the Government

Accountability Office and the Pentagon's own inspector general testify to this.[6]

Along with immensely profitable war contracts comes increased income inequality and the defunding of public services. The impoverishment of public services is not only one of the costs of empire; it is one of the *goals*. The imperial rulers wage war not only against people in foreign lands but against their own populace as well, diminishing their demands, expectations, and sense of entitlement.

There are those who say that empires are "economically irrational" affairs because they cost more than they bring in. The British spent more in India than they were able to extract, and they extracted quite a bit. So too with the Americans in the Philippines and in Central America. But the people who pay the costs of empire are not the same as those who reap its rewards. As Thorstein Veblen pointed out in 1904, the gains of empire flow into the hands of the privileged business class, the large overseas investors, while the costs are extracted from the general treasury, that is, from "the industry of the rest of the people."[7] The same has been true in regard to Iraq: US taxpayers have carried the costs and are paying the debt that the war brought, while Halliburton, Blackwater, and a hundred other corporations reap the fat no-bid contracts and corrupt dealings, almost all of it not audited.[8]

Global Military Dominance

If US policy is respectful of other peoples' sovereignty and needs, then we might wonder why US leaders find it necessary to engage in a relentless push for global military domination. Since the 1990s they have been guided by various versions of a policy plan put together by Dick Cheney (soon to become U.S. vice-president) with Paul Wolfowitz and Colin Powell, who respectively became secretaries of Defense and State. The agenda was for the United States to exercise unilateral rule over the world. As one writer put it:

[The plan] calls for the United States to maintain its overwhelming military superiority and prevent new rivals from rising up to challenge it on the world stage. It calls for dominion over friends and enemies alike. It says not that the United States must be more powerful, but that it must be absolutely powerful.[9]

The United States presides over an armed planetary force of a magnitude never before seen in human history. As listed by the Department of Defense, this force includes over a half-million troops stationed at over 700 military bases around the planet and many more within the fifty states, including numerous secret ones that go uncounted along with unusually large bases recently constructed in Central Asia, Iraq, Colombia, and Kosovo.[10] In 2009 a democratically elected progressive government in Ecuador closed down the last US military base on its soil, claiming it was a violation of that country's sovereignty. Both Ecuador and Bolivia now have a ban on foreign bases written into their constitutions.

The US global war machine boasts an arsenal of over 5,000 strategic nuclear warheads[11] and 22,000 tactical ones, along with a naval strike force greater in total tonnage and firepower than all the other navies of the world combined, sailing every ocean and making port at every continent. Bomber squadrons and long-range missiles can deliver enough explosive force to cripple the infrastructures of entire countries anywhere on the globe. US rapid deployment forces have a firepower in conventional weaponry vastly superior to any other nation's force. Satellites and US spy planes conduct a surveillance that blankets the entire planet. Recent years brought a skyrocketing increase in military spending for the "war on terrorism."[12]

By 2011 the Obama administration was planning to deploy, on US soil, a new class of weapon capable of reaching any corner of the planet in less than an hour. The weapon will deliver a conventional warhead of enormous explosive force at pinpoint accuracy and phenomenally high speed, mimicking the destructive impact of a nuclear warhead and greatly diminishing America's reliance on its nuclear arsenal.[13]

The Pentagon has also developed an arsenal of space weaponry that runs the risk of sparking an arms race in outer space, including the unmanned X-37 space plane now circling Earth. The goal is to develop space vehicles that can hit terrestrial and outer space targets (including satellites) and send reconnaissance and attack drones back into the atmosphere.[14] By 2010 the Obama administration had stated its commitment to "equitable" arms control measures and "openness and transparency" among nations in conducting operations in outer space, while continuing a claim "to use space for national security activities."[15]

Despite the development of new weaponry, Washington showed no readiness to diminish its aging stockpile of tactical nuclear missiles in Europe. Requests by several NATO allies to cut back were rejected by the White House. As one reporter noted, "Many analysts consider these weapons a dangerous relic of the cold war, expensive to safeguard and deadly if they fell into the wrong hands."[16]

In the realm of conventional arms also, the United States has exercised an unmatched global reach, accounting for almost 70 percent of the world's conventional arms sales. Since World War II, Washington has given hundreds of billions of dollars in military aid to train and equip the troops and internal security forces of more than eighty countries, the purpose being not to defend these nations from outside invasion but to protect ruling oligarchs and multinational corporate investors from the dangers of domestic insurgency.

How do we know this? By observing that:

- With few exceptions there is no evidence suggesting that these various régimes have ever been threatened by neighboring countries.
- There is a great deal of evidence that the US-supported military and security forces and death squads in many of these countries

have been repeatedly used to destroy popular reformist movements and insurgencies within the countries themselves, ones that advocate egalitarian redistributive ("leftist") politics.

- Most "friendly" recipient régimes have supported the integration of their economies into a global system of corporate domination, opening themselves to foreign penetration on "free trade" terms singularly favorable to transnational investors.[17]

Note also the Pentagon's wide-ranging incursions into everyday life in America. The military exercises a censorial role in the making of Hollywood war films and cultivates connections with the World Wrestling Entertainment, NASCAR, Starbucks, and companies that deal with everything from iPods to Oakley sunglasses. The military is contractually involved in hundreds of scientific research projects, including such exotic and frightful undertakings as creating "cyborg insects" that can be remotely controlled and armed with bio-weapons. The Pentagon also is devising ways to socialize youngsters into having a receptive "culture of cool" response to the military by making friends on MySpace and other cyberspace connections and promotions.[18]

After the Red Menace

For decades we were told that a huge military establishment was necessary to contain an expansionist world communist movement with its headquarters in Moscow (or sometimes Beijing). The United States and other western capitalist nations formed the North Atlantic Treaty Organization (NATO) in 1949 supposedly to serve as a bulwark against the threat of a Soviet invasion across Europe. Evidence of such a threat was never forthcoming.[19] Still the "NATO shield" was put together, consisting of a massive build-up of military forces throughout Western Europe operating in effect under the hegemony of the United States.

But after the overthrow of the Soviet Union and other Eastern European communist nations, Washington made no move to dismantle NATO. Instead of being abolished, NATO was expanded to include nations that reached across Eastern Europe right to Russia's border. In trying to convince us that we still needed NATO, policymakers and editorialists let fly a variety of arguments.

First, we heard that NATO is a relative bargain since the United States pays only 25 percent of its cost—as if this spoke to its purpose or political value.

Second, NATO can be used as a collective force for interventions without being stymied by a UN veto, as might happen when Washington seeks a United Nations mandate for war and invasion against some country. In other words, the United States has a freer hand operating through NATO than through the United Nations. Thus when the UN Security Council (because of Russian and Chinese vetoes) refused to cooperate with the destruction of Yugoslavia, Washington just enlisted NATO.[20]

Third, we are told by one mainstream newspaper that "NATO is committed to defending countries that share a commitment to democracy and free enterprise."[21]

Do we still need NATO? Actually the US public never needed NATO. The Soviet Red Army had neither the interest nor the capacity to invade Western Europe after World War II; State Department studies have admitted as much. Does that mean NATO has been senseless or useless? Not at all; it is a valuable tool to lock the Western European countries into the US imperial system, just as it is now doing to the newly capitalized Eastern European countries.

After the overthrow of the Soviet Union and the other Eastern European communist nations, all Cold War weapons programs in the United States continued in production, with new ones being added all the time, including plans to conduct war from outer space. In short time the White House and Pentagon began issuing jeremiads about a whole host of new enemies—for some unexplained reason previously overlooked—who posed a mortal threat to the United States, including "dangerous rogue states" like Libya with its menacing rag-tag army of 50,000.

The Newly Conjured Menace

Since the 1990s, a favorite villain conjured by US rulers to strike fear into the hearts of the American public has been the *Islamic terrorist,* who supposedly is part of a vast international network named Al Qaeda, headed by the diabolical Osama bin Laden, master of trained operatives in over forty countries. No hard evidence of such a wide-reaching coordinated terrorist foe has been found.[22] Usually left unmentioned is how the United States helped organize, finance, and mobilize the Islamic militants to fight a regressive war against revolutionary Afghanistan during the Soviet intervention into that country.[23]

To be sure, real terrorists do exist, a sparse scattering of poorly organized grouplets. They must be stopped before they can commit their wanton acts. But this gives no government—not even the one in Washington—license to bomb and destroy whole countries. Such massive military aggression delivers a much greater destruction than anything done by the jihadists and is destined to *create* rather than eliminate Islamic terrorists.

This seems to be the view held by Osama bin Laden and his followers, who see themselves involved in a defensive war against a merciless aggressor. They seem less impelled by some blind hatred and envy of America and more by a desire to get the American empire off their backs. They hate the empire because of the terrible things it does to them, their homelands, and their region of the world, bringing them exploitation, death, and destruction on a grand scale.[24]

3

Why Rulers Seek Global Dominion

How do we divine the motives of US leaders when they intervene in other countries? There is no shortage of lamenting about all the terrible and difficult situations that US leaders get into around the world, a lamentation made all the more pathetic for being unaccompanied by any critical analysis of the interests being served by such involvements.

Determining Intent

Human motives are impossible to observe in any empirical way. We can view behavior and listen to utterances, but we cannot directly observe the actual *intent* that is attributed to such things. No one has ever seen a motive as such. Intent can only be inferred or imputed.

While people profess all sorts of intentions, they also are capable of outrageous deception, including self-deception. How then can we determine, or dare presume, what might be their actual motives?

The problem becomes crucial when dealing with political leaders, many of whom make it difficult to divine the intentions behind their actions. Some of us maintain that the overriding purpose of global interventionism is to promote the interests of transnational corporations and make the world safe for global free-market capitalism and imperialism. As noted earlier, imperialism is what empires do. It is the process whereby the rulers of one country use economic and military power to expropriate the land, labor, markets, and natural resources of less powerful countries on behalf of wealthy interests at home and abroad.

Washington policymakers are the last to admit that they engage in such a process. They claim that their interventions abroad are propelled by an intent to defend our national security or other unspecified "US interests," or the intent is to fight terrorism, protect human rights, oppose tyranny, prevent genocide, bring democracy to other peoples, maintain peace and stability in various regions, and protect weaker nations from aggressors.

Are we to accept these noble claims at face value? If not, how can we demonstrate that they are often false and that the motive *we* critics ascribe is the real agenda? How can we determine intent if intent is not readily susceptible to direct observation and policymakers can make claim to almost any noble motivation? How can we determine that interventionism is engendered by imperialist concerns rather than, say, humanitarian and democratic ones?

First of all, we can look for *patterns of intervention.* Are there any consistencies in US overseas intercessions? If so, what kinds of governments and political movements do US leaders support? What kinds do they oppose and wish to subject to *régime change*? And what political-economic goals do they pursue when intervening? Rather than characterizing US policy as befuddled and contradictory, we observe that it is remarkably consistent in services rendered on behalf of transnational economic domination. Other policy considerations do come into play during times of intervention, but there is no reason to treat them as mutually exclusive of global business interests, and no reason to ignore the latter.

Bolstering the Right-Wing Autocrats

The motives of the US national security state can be revealed in part by noting whom it supports and whom it attacks. By the "US national security state" I mean the Executive Office of the White House, the National Security Council (NSC), National Security Agency, Central Intelligence Agency (CIA), Federal Bureau of Investigation (FBI), and other such units that are engaged in surveillance, suppression, covert action, and forceful interventions abroad and at home. Also included are the various monitoring committees set up by the NSC, composed of top players from the Department of State and Department of Defense (the Pentagon), the CIA, the Joint Chiefs of Staff, and the White House.

The efforts of these highly placed government bodies are supplemented by ostensibly nongovernmental groups such as the Council on Foreign Relations, the Trilateral Commission, the Bilderberg Conference, the Bohemian Grove, and other formal and informal elite groups populated by political leaders, policy specialists, bankers, CEOs, big investors, leading publicists, and a sprinkling of academic acolytes. The Americans among them are the individuals who inhabit the upper circles of US power, who become the secretaries of State, Defense, Treasury, Commerce, and heads of the CIA and the National Security Council, in that revolving door between Washington and Wall Street.[1]

huh?

Q

These US leaders have consistently supported rightist régimes and organizations and opposed leftist ones. The terms *right* and *left* are frequently bandied about but seldom specifically defined by policymakers or media commentators—and with good reason. The power of a label is in its being left undefined, allowing it to have an abstracted built-in demonizing impact that precludes rational examination of its political content. To explicate the actual political-economic content of leftist governments and movements is to reveal their egalitarian and usually democratic goals, making it much harder to demonize them.

The Left, as I would define it, encompasses those individuals, organizations, and governments that advocate egalitarian, redistributive policies and human services benefiting the common people and infringing upon the privileged interests of the wealthy propertied classes.

The Right also is involved in redistributive politics, but the distribution goes the other way, in an upward direction advancing the privileges of private capital and the wealthy few. Rightist governments and groups, including fascist ones, are dedicated to using the labor, markets, and natural resources of countries as so much fodder for the enrichment of the owning classes. In almost every country including our own, rightist groups, parties, or governments advocate privatization and deregulation of the economy, along with tax and spending programs, wage and investment practices, and methods of police and military control that primarily benefit those who receive the bulk of their income from investments and property, at the expense of those who live off wages, salaries, fees, and pensions. That is what usually distinguishes the Right from the Left.

In just about each instance, rightist forces abroad are deemed by US opinion makers to be "friendly to the West," a coded term for "pro–free market" and "pro-capitalist." Conversely, leftist ones are labeled as hostile, "antidemocratic," "anti-American," and "anti-West," when in fact they are anti–corporate capital and against the privileges of the super rich.

While claiming to be motivated by a dedication to human rights and democracy, US leaders have supported some of the most notorious right-wing autocracies in history—régimes that have pursued policies favoring wealthy transnational corporations at the expense of local producers and working people; régimes that have tortured, killed, or otherwise maltreated large numbers of their more resistant citizens, as in (at one time or another) Chad, Pakistan, Turkey, Indonesia, Honduras, Peru, Colombia, Argentina, El Salvador, Guatemala, Haiti, the Philippines, Chile (under Pinochet), Cuba (under Batista), Congo/Zaire (under Mobutu), Nicaragua (under Somoza), Iran (under the Shah), Iraq (under Saddam Hussein until 1990), Morocco (under King Hassan), and Portugal (under Salazar), to offer an incomplete listing.

US imperialists have assisted *counterrevolutionary insurgencies* that have perpetrated brutal bloodletting against civilian populations; for example, Unita in Angola, Renamo in Mozambique, the *contras* in Nicaragua, the Khmer Rouge (during the 1980s) in Cambodia, the mujahedeen and then the Taliban in Afghanistan (in the 1980s and 1990s against a Soviet-supported reformist government), and (in 1999–2000) the drug-dealing Albanian Kosovo Liberation Army in Yugoslavia (originally deemed a terrorist organization by the US State Department). All this is a matter of public record, although it is seldom if ever reported in the US media.

Support for rightists extends to Nazism itself. After World War II, US leaders and their western capitalist allies did little to eradicate fascism from Europe, except for putting some of the top Nazi leaders on trial at Nuremberg. In short time, many former Nazis and their active collaborators were back in the saddle in Germany.[2] Hundreds of Nazi war criminals found a haven in the United States, either living in comfortable anonymity or employed by US intelligence agencies during the Cold War.[3]

In France, too, very few Vichy collaborators were purged. "No one of any rank was seriously punished for his or her role in the roundup and deportation of Jews to Nazi camps."[4] US military authorities also restored fascist collaborators to power in various Far East nations. In South Korea, for instance, police trained by the fascist Japanese occupation force were used immediately after the war to suppress left democratic forces. The South Korean Army was commanded by officers who had served (proudly) in the Imperial Japanese Army, some of whom had been guilty of horrid war crimes in the Philippines and China.[5]

In Italy, within a year after the war, almost all Italian fascists were released from prison while hundreds of communists and other leftist partisans who had been valiantly fighting the Nazi occupation were incarcerated. Allied authorities initiated most of these measures.[6] From 1945 to 1975, US government agencies gave an estimated $75 million to right-wing organizations in Italy, including some with close ties to the neofascist Movimento Sociale Italiano (MSI).

Suppressing the Leftist Rebels and Reformers

When trying to determine the intentions of policymakers, we should look not only at whom they support but whom they attack. US rulers have targeted just about all leftist governments, parties, leaders, political movements, and popular insurgencies—that is, any political entity that attempts to initiate equitable reforms, egalitarian programs for the common people, restraints on corporate capital, and self-development for their own countries.

Consider once more the parliamentary social democracies in Italy and Western Europe. From 1969 to 1974, high-ranking elements in Italian military and civilian intelligence agencies, along with various secret and highly placed neofascist groups, embarked upon a campaign of terror and sabotage known as the "strategy of tension," involving a series of kidnappings, assassinations, and bombings (*i stragi*), including the explosion that massacred eighty-five people and wounded some two hundred in the Bologna train station in August 1980. Fueled by international security agencies including the CIA, the terrorism was directed against the growing popularity of the democratic parliamentary left. The objective was to "combat by any means necessary the electoral gains of the Italian Communist Party" and create enough terror to destabilize the multiparty social democracy and replace it with an authoritarian "presidential republic," or in any case "a stronger and more stable executive." Deeply implicated in this terrorist campaign, the CIA refused to cooperate with an Italian parliamentary commission investigating *i stragi* in 1995. [7]

In the 1980s, scores of leftists were murdered in Germany, Belgium, and elsewhere in Western Europe by extreme rightists in the service of state security agencies. As with the "strategy of tension" in Italy, the US corporate-owned media largely ignored these acts of right-wing terrorism—while giving prominent play to tiny and far less effective left terrorist grouplets found in Italy and West Germany.

In Italy, as long as the Communist Party retained imposing strength in parliament and within the labor unions, US policymakers worked with centrist alternatives such as the Christian Democrats and the anticommunist Italian Socialist Party. With communism in decline by the 1990s, US leaders began to lend more open encouragement to extreme rightist forces. In 1994 and again in 2001, national elections were won by the National Alliance, a coalition of neofascists, ultraconservatives, and northern separatists headed by ultra-rightist media tycoon Silvio Berlusconi.

The National Alliance played on resentments regarding unemployment, taxes, and immigration. It attempted to convince people that government was the enemy—especially its social service sector (as do reactionary elements in the Republican Party in the United States), all the while preaching the virtues of the free market, and pursuing tax and spending measures that redistributed income upward. US leaders and mainstream media have had not a harsh word to say about these Italian crypto-fascists.

The methods of domination employed by the US imperium to subvert and defeat reformist and leftist governments are as varied and ruthless as the opportunities of intervention may allow. Here is an incomplete listing:

- Bribe and penetrate a government's internal security units and intelligence agencies, providing them with counterinsurgency training and technology. Bribe top political and military leaders, and other power players, at times giving them a share of the drug trade payoffs in their region.
- Collude with organized crime in gun running, narcotics trafficking, and special (illegal) operations.
- Maintain secret prisons and interrogation centers; provide instruments of torture, train torturers, and supervise torture sessions.
- Disrupt and destroy protest groups and other popular organizations that support reform. Organize death squads to assassinate especially effective progressive leaders and organizers.
- Recruit and finance mercenary armies and paramilitary units to conduct assassinations, disappearances, massacres, and terror bombings. Wage *low-intensity warfare* (low-scale wars of attrition) that can continue for years, including strikes against "soft targets" such as schools, clinics, farm cooperatives, public venues, and whole villages.
- Incite, arm, and finance retrograde ethnic separatists and supremacists who act as a divisive element and rise against the targeted government.
- Propagate endless waves of false propaganda and move toward monopolizing world media. Buy up or secretly subsidize existing radio and television stations, periodicals, and publishing houses, or finance new ones.
- Sabotage and suppress dissident media by threat and intimidation, police actions, killing journalists, and destroying media

sites, sometimes with aerial attacks, as done in Yugoslavia, Bosnia, and Iraq.

- Secretly subsidize conservative academic research and mainstream political scholarship; promote and finance depoliticized forms of art and literature. Provide awards; arrange exhibitions, guest lectures, and teaching opportunities; and free trips abroad designed to bribe, win over, and politically neutralize writers, academics, artists, and journalists from the targeted countries.
- Undermine the targeted country's indigenous cultures with US corporate consumer and entertainment products.
- Secretly finance compliant labor unions to undermine more militant radical ones. Finance conservative religious proselytizers, lecturers, and various nongovernmental organizations (NGOs).
- Rig elections; finance and advise collaborationist political parties and candidates while perpetrating disruptive ploys and other dirty tricks against their opponents.
- Impose crippling embargoes and trade sanctions that damage the living standards of targeted régimes. Draw them into heavy deficit spending and debt peonage to paralyze their development, forcing them to endure austerity programs in order to meet debt payments. [8]

Enemies Without End

US leaders profess a dedication to democracy. Yet over the past six decades, democratically elected reformist governments and revolutionary governments and movements, guilty of supporting egalitarian economic programs, have been attacked by their own military forces (secretly infiltrated and funded by the United States), or by US-supported mercenary forces and "dirty tricks" operatives dedicated to rolling back reforms and opening their countries to foreign corporate investors and private market "solutions"—such as happened at one time or another in Afghanistan, Angola, Argentina, Bolivia, Brazil, Cambodia, Chad, Chile, Congo, Cuba, Cyprus, Dominican Republic, East Timor, Ecuador, Egypt, Ethiopia, Fiji Islands, Greece (twice), Guatemala, Guyana, Haiti (twice), Honduras, Indonesia (under Sukarno), Iran, Jamaica, Lebanon, Libya, Mozambique, Nicaragua, Peru, Portugal, South Yemen, Syria, Thailand, Uruguay, Western Sahara, and others.[9]

Since World War II, US military forces have *invaded or launched aerial assaults* against Afghanistan, Cambodia, Dominican Republic, Grenada, Iraq (twice), Laos, Lebanon, Libya, North Korea, Panama, Somalia, Vietnam, Pakistan, and Yugoslavia—a record of military aggression unmatched by any communist or "terrorist" government in history.[10] (All these listings are incomplete.) In some instances, neoimperialism has been replaced with an old-fashioned direct colonialist occupation, or attempted occupation, as in Bosnia, Kosovo, Macedonia (and for more than a century, Puerto Rico), and more recently Iraq and Afghanistan.

Even before World War II, the US imperium was engaged in violent interventions. US military forces waged a bloody war of attrition in the Philippines from 1898 to 1903. US expeditionary forces fought in China along with other western armies to suppress the Boxer Rebellion and keep the Chinese under the heel of European and North American colonialists. Along with over a dozen other capitalist nations, the United States invaded revolutionary Russia from 1918 to 1921. US Marines invaded and occupied Nicaragua in 1912 and again in 1926 to 1933; Cuba, 1898 to 1902; Mexico, 1914 and 1916; Panama, 1903 to 1914; Haiti, 1915 to 1934; and Honduras six times between 1911 and 1925.

Governments that strive for any kind of economic independence, or apply some significant portion of their budgets to public-sector, not-for-profit services that benefit the people and bring self-development, are the ones most likely to feel the wrath of US intervention. The designated "enemy" can be:

- a *populist military government* as in Panama under Omar Torrijos (and even under Manuel Noriega), Egypt under Gamal Abdul Nasser, Peru under Juan Velasco, Portugal under the MFA (leftist military officers), and Venezuela under Hugo Chávez (the latter democratically elected president several times)
- a *Christian socialist government* as in Nicaragua under the Sandinistas (democratically elected after the revolutionary overthrow of the Somoza dictatorship)
- a *social democracy* as in Chile under Salvador Allende, Jamaica under Michael Manley, Greece under Andreas Papandreou, Cyprus under Mihail Makarios, and the Dominican Republic under Juan Bosch
- an *anticolonialist radical reform government* as in the Congo under the democratically elected Patrice Lumumba
- a *Marxist-Leninist government* as in Cuba, Vietnam, and North Korea
- an *Islamic revolutionary order* as in Libya under Muammar al-Qaddafi
- a *conservative Islamic* government that maintains some economic nationalism and minimal populist programs as in Iran under Mahmoud Ahmadinejad, or even
- a *conservative militarist régime* as in Iraq under Saddam Hussein should it maintain an independent course on oil quotas and a state-owned economy[11]

In sum, we can determine the motives that impel US leaders by observing the following: just about all the countries designated as *friendly* to the United States are régimes that maintain economic systems integrated into the US sphere of corporate global domination. Just about all the countries designated as *unfriendly* have at one time or another resisted being drawn into the US sphere of corporate domination.

US-supported military and paramilitary forces, death squads, and police have been repeatedly used to destroy reformist movements, labor unions, peasant organizations, and popular insurgencies that advocate some kind of an egalitarian redistributive politics in both the "unfriendly" countries and, when necessary, the "friendly" ones as well.

Our political and corporate leaders repeatedly tell us that the world is a relentlessly hostile place. They see enemies everywhere, largely because their own imperial interests put them in conflict with so many. About half a century ago, the celebrated conservative military figure General Douglas MacArthur had this to say about those who profess to guard our ramparts: "Our country is now geared to an arms economy which was bred in an artificially induced psychosis of war hysteria and nurtured upon an incessant propaganda of fear."[12]

For the global interventionists to insure the blessings of an untrammeled "free market" corporate paradise, they must maintain plutocratic control of the planet. To accomplish this, they must rally public opinion behind them through patriotic pride and fear of alien dangers. Once the people fear for their survival, they are ready to hand over their tax dollars and even their democratic rights to their rulers—who are presumed to know best.

4

Deliberate Design

THE GOAL OF US REACTIONARY RULERS is the Third Worldization of the entire world including Europe and North America, a New World Order in which capital rules supreme with no public sector services or labor unions to speak of; no prosperous, literate, effectively organized working class or highly educated middle class with rising expectations and a strong sense of entitlement; no public medical care, pension funds, occupational safety, or environmental and consumer protections, or any of the other insufferable things that might cut into profits and lead to a more egalitarian distribution of life chances.

The Third Worldization of Eastern Europe

Only in a few rare cases have US leaders treated leftist governments or forces in a "friendly" fashion: Yugoslavia as a buffer state during the Cold War, the Khmer Rouge killers (if they could be considered leftist) against the socialist government in Cambodia during the 1980s, and China and Vietnam today as they allow business investments in their "enterprise zones." In such instances Washington's support has been dictated by temporary expediencies or the promise, as in the case of China and Vietnam, that the countries are moving toward a capitalist system.

In the period after World War II, US policymakers sent assistance to Third World nations and put forth a Marshall Plan for Western Europe, grudgingly accepting reforms that produced social benefits for the working classes of various countries. They did this because of the Cold War competition with the Soviet Union and the strong showing of communist parties in European elections and in the control of trade unions, especially in France and Italy.[1]

But today with the communist nations having disappeared, there is no need to make concessions to workers in Western Europe. There being no competing lure, Third World peoples—and working populations everywhere—are subjected to the rollback of benefits and wages that had been won through years of democratic struggle.

One can judge the intentions of policymakers by what they do to countries drawn into the Western orbit. For decades we were told that the Cold War was a contest between freedom and an expansionist communism, with nothing said about the expansionist interests of global capitalism. But immediately after communism was overthrown in the USSR and Eastern Europe, US rulers began intimating that there was something more on their agenda than just free elections for the former "captive nations"—namely free markets.[2] Of what use was political democracy, the free marketeers seemed to be saying, if it allowed the retention of an economy that was socialistic or even social democratic? To the US globalists, a country's political system weighed less than the kind of economic system it had.

Getting rid of communism, it became clear, meant getting rid of public ownership of industry and most of the public sector in general, reducing the social wage to as close to zero as possible, and installing an untrammeled free market economy.

Throughout the former Soviet Union and Eastern Europe, post-communism "reforms" and newly installed private-market governments brought high unemployment and a severe decline in the standard of living, specifically as follows:

- The free market governments eliminated price controls and sub-sidies for food, housing, transportation, clothing, and utilities.
- They abolished job guarantees and workplace benefits and in many instances forbade workplace political activities by labor unions.
- They privatized many medical services, cut back on medical benefits, and decreased support for public education.
- They sold off publicly owned lands and news media at bargain prices along with state-owned oil, gas, iron, coal, and transport resources. Profitable and competitive mines, factories, and energy systems were in effect stolen by the new gang-related oligarchs.[3] Numerous other industries were simply shut down.

There was a massive transfer of public capital into the coffers of private owners amounting to over a trillion dollars. Contrary to a common view propagated on both the Left and Right, the new Russian oligarchs were not former Communist Party commissars who merely shifted from public to private control but mafia-style private groups unconnected to the government, appearing on the national scene in unprecedented numbers. "Without exception," notes James Petras, "the transfers of property were achieved through gangster tactics—assassinations, massive theft ... of state resources, illicit stock manipulation and buyouts."[4] A kleptocracy in progress.

Throughout the former Soviet Union and Eastern Europe, this process of privatization by plunder and intimidation, described in

ECONOMIC CYCLES

the western press as "reforms," brought severe economic recession and a high rate of unemployment, along with a dramatic drop in educational and literacy standards; serious deterioration in health care and all other public services; skyrocketing infant mortality; and a sharp increase in crime, suicide, homelessness, beggary, prostitution, and drug addiction—all resulting in plummeting life expectancy rates.[5] In 2010, twenty years after the installment of free market capitalism in Eastern Europe, these distressing conditions were as bad as ever. Countries like Latvia (having experienced full employment under communism) still suffered about 20 percent unemployment, and those were only the official figures, which tend to understate the real situation by leaving all sorts of down-and-out cohorts uncounted.[6]

In former communist countries like Russia, Poland, Hungary, and Romania, crypto-fascist and anti-Semitic organizations surfaced. Leftist dissidents were jailed, their parties outlawed, their publications silenced, and their labor unions banned. Laws were passed in some of the countries prohibiting criticisms of capitalism, the advocacy of socialism, and the propagation of "class hatred."[7]

One of the former communist nations, Belarus, failed to convert fully to the free market paradise. Belarus was ruled by freely elected President Alexander Lukashenko, who dared to kick out the International Monetary Fund (IMF) and World Bank and refused to privatize and deregulate the entire economy, preferring to pursue policies on behalf of low-income people, rural workers, and the elderly. The Organization for Security and Cooperation (OSCE), which includes the United States and some fifty other nations, has the self-appointed task of overseeing the transformation away from socialism in former communist nations. The OSCE succeeded in organizing the splintered opposition to Lukashenko into a single voting bloc that favored the free market. In 2001 the *New York Times* admitted that the CIA also was working with the Belarussian opposition.[8]

Other Rollbacks

One method of imposing régime change upon a dissident country is by direct military invasion. Consider what happened to revolutionary Grenada. In 1983, US forces invaded the tiny sovereign nation of Grenada (population 102,000) in violation of all international law. The invasion could not be denied, but what of the motive? The Reagan administration justified the assault by claiming that it was a rescue operation on behalf of American students whose safety was being threatened at a Grenadian medical school; and worse still, the island was being turned into a Soviet-Cuban launching base "to export terror and undermine democracy."[9]

When it became evident that these charges were without foundation, some critics determined that the White House had been unduly alarmist and misguided. But, again, the fact that officials offer misleading rationales is no reason to conclude that they are themselves misled. It may be that they have other motives that they prefer not to enunciate.

In fact, the policy toward Grenada was quite rational and successful, given the Reagan administration's devotion to counterrevolutionary free market goals. Under the New Jewel revolutionary government in Grenada, free milk and other foodstuffs were being distributed to the needy, as were materials for home improvement. Grade school and secondary education were free for everyone for the first time. Free health clinics were opened in the countryside, thanks mostly to assistance rendered by Cuban doctors. Measures were taken in support of equal pay and legal status for women. The government leased unused land to establish farm cooperatives and turned agriculture away from cash-crop exports and toward self-sufficient food production.[10]

The US counterrevolutionary occupation put an immediate end to almost all these government-sponsored programs. In the years that followed the US invasion, unemployment in Grenada reached new heights and poverty new depths. Domestic cooperatives were shut down or starved out. Farm families were displaced to make way for golf courses. The corporate-controlled tourist industry boomed. Grenada was once more firmly locked into a privatized Third World poverty.

The same process occurred after the US invaded Panama in December 1989, supposedly to apprehend Manuel Noriega, described by the White House and the US press as a drug-dealing dictator. With Noriega and his leftist military deposed and the US military firmly in control, conditions in that country deteriorated sharply. Unemployment, already high because of the US embargo, climbed to 35 percent as drastic layoffs were imposed on the public sector. Pension rights and other work benefits were abolished. Government subsidies were eliminated and services were privatized. The US invaders shut down publicly owned media and jailed a number of Panamanian editors and reporters who were critical of the invasion. The US military arrested labor union leaders and removed some 150 progressive labor leaders from their elected positions within their unions. Crime, poverty, drug trafficking, and homelessness increased dramatically.[11] Free market Third Worldization was firmly reinstated in Panama, all in the name of restoring "democracy."

Underlying Consistencies

US foreign policy is often criticized by confused liberals for being "self-contradictory." For instance, they point out that communist Cuba has been subjected to every hostile stratagem, including travel and trade embargoes, sabotage, and expeditionary invasion, while communist China—which has committed numerous human rights violations—has been granted "most favored nation" trading status. US policymakers repeatedly have tried to assure the fundamentalist hawks in Congress that we should not impose a political litmus test on China. But one is regularly imposed on Cuba. This is not a sensibly consistent policy, the liberal critics say.

Presidents inherit political situations and must pave their own way for others.

In fact, it is quite consistent. Behind the apparently contradictory policies toward China and Cuba rests the same underlying commitment to capital accumulation. China has opened itself to private capital and free market "reforms," including "enterprise zones" wherein western investors can take advantage of the country's huge labor supply with no worry about occupation standards or other restrictive regulations— although in July 2010, for the first time, wildcat strikes did occur in China against foreign employers. And today the professed goal of the Chinese government is to improve the standard of living of its own population and assist by trade and aid the developing nations of the world. (Indeed, the more successful China proves to be in its internal development and its relations with Third World nations, the more it is again becoming a target of western elites, defamed as a mortal threat to US national security.)

Cuba so far has refused to go down the free market road, although it appears in late 2010 to be moving toward a partially privatized economy in the service sector. When the Cuban government abolishes the social wage that serves the common populace, when it eliminates its totally free public health system, when it privatizes the factories and lands and allows the productive wealth to be pocketed by rich corporate owners, and removes all labor protections for workers, then it will have come full circle, being once more under capitalist vassal-state servitude. And then most surely will Havana be embraced by Washington, as have the ex-communist newly established free market nations in Eastern Europe.

[handwritten margin note: Yes, and people are in rafts leaving Cuba to come to the U.S.!]

[handwritten across page: AAAARGH!!!]

When the Truth Slips Out

It should not go unnoticed that leaders occasionally do verbalize their dedication to making the world safe for the transnational corporate system. At such times words seem to speak louder than actions, for the words are an admission of the real motives behind the action.

In 1953, for instance, President Dwight Eisenhower uttered a forbidden truth in his State of the Union message: "A serious and explicit purpose of our foreign policy [is] the encouragement of a hospitable climate for [corporate] investment in foreign nations."[12] In 1990, General Alfred Gray, commandant of the US Marines, observed that the United States must have "unimpeded access" to "established and developing economic markets throughout the world."[13]

US opinion makers treat capitalism as inseparable from democracy. However, rather than coming right out and saying capitalism, they prefer softened terms like "free market," "market economy," "economic reforms," and "free market democracy." So President Clinton announced before the United Nations on September 27, 1993: "Our overriding purpose is to expand and strengthen the world's community of market-based democracies."[14]

In a similar vein, the *New York Times,* supportive of the repressive and murderous measures perpetrated against parliamentary democracy by Russian president Boris Yeltsin in 1993, opined that "Yeltsin remains the best hope for democracy and a market economy in Russia."[15] For many years, one of the most pronounced cheerleaders of the US imperium was Samuel P. Huntington, Harvard professor and former CIA advisor, who wrote that the United States is the "only major power whose national identity is defined by a set of universal political and economic values," specifically "liberty, democracy, equality, private property, and markets."[16]

US rulers frequently inject themselves into elections in other lands, lavishly funding rightist elements that disrupt egalitarian movements or help overthrow leftist reformist governments. Elections can serve as a means of régime change, acting as a legitimating cloak for capitalist restoration. But when popular forces successfully utilize electoral democracy as a defense against untrammeled capitalism, democracy runs into trouble. In this latter instance, rather than being wedded to each other, capitalism and democracy are on a fatal collision course, as US leaders demonstrated in Guatemala in 1953, Chile in 1973, Greece in 1967, Indonesia in 1965, Yugoslavia in 2000, and a score of other countries in which US funds and guns were used in great abundance to overthrow democratically elected governments.

Over the past two decades US policymakers have explicitly demanded "free market reforms" in all the former communist nations of Eastern Europe. We no longer have to impute such intent to them. In 1996 Lawrence Summers, serving as President Clinton's undersecretary of the treasury, proudly remarked: "Our ideology, capitalism, is in ascendancy everywhere."[17] In 2000, the White House hailed the Stability Pact for South Eastern Europe (an organization of about fifteen nations plus the European Union) for planning to create "vibrant market economies" in the Balkans. That same year, the Overseas Private Investment Corporation (OPIC) inaugurated a fund to be managed by Soros Private Funds Management. Its purpose, as stated by the US embassy in Macedonia, was "to provide capital for new business development, expansion and privatization." Meanwhile, the Agency for International Development (USAID) planned—in its own words—"assistance programs ... to advance Montenegro toward a free market economy."[18]

In April 2001, according to the London *Financial Times*, the newly installed conservative rulers of Yugoslavia, beneficiaries of millions of dollars in US electoral funds, launched "a comprehensive privatization program as part of economic reforms introduced following the overthrow of former president Slobodan Milošević." This included the sale of more than 7,000 publicly owned or worker controlled companies to private investors at giveaway prices.[19]

Secrecy and "Innocent Incompetence"

To say, as many critics do, that US national security leaders know more, intend more, and do more than they let on is not to claim they are omnipotent or omniscient. Critics such as I argue that—although mistakes are made and unintended consequences certainly can arise—US policy is not habitually misguided and bungling. Rather, it is impressively consistent and cohesive, a deadly success for the interests it represents. Those who see the US imperium as chronically befuddled are themselves revealing their own befuddlement.

Sometimes the policymakers themselves seize upon incompetence as a cover. In 1986 it was discovered that the Reagan administration was running a covert operation to bypass Congress (and the law), using funds from secret arms sales to Iran to finance counterrevolutionary mercenaries (the "contras") in Nicaragua and probably GOP electoral campaigns at home. President Reagan admitted full knowledge of the arms sales but claimed he had no idea what happened to the money. He was asking us to believe that these operations were being conducted by subordinates, including his own top advisors, without being cleared by him. Reagan publicly criticized himself for his slipshod managerial style and lack of administrative control over his staff. His admission of incompetence was eagerly embraced by various pundits who prefer to see their leaders as suffering from innocent ignorance rather than designing deception. Subsequent testimony by his subordinates, however, revealed that Reagan was not as dumb as he was pretending to be, and that he had played a deciding role in the entire Iran-contra affair.[20]

The same holds for President George W. Bush, whose tendency to flub words added to the facile conclusion that he was witless and stupid. In fact, Bush knew what he was doing and did what he wanted. Consider the following:

- On behalf of the super rich, Bush succeeded in greatly diminishing the progressive inheritance tax, at the same time reducing corporate taxes to nominal amounts and undermining federal controls and regulations on business.
- Bush stacked the federal courts with young right-wing activist ideologues, expanded the autocratic powers of the "unitary

executive," operated in secrecy and blocked transparency, and rolled back civil liberties under the guise of fighting "terrorism."

- Bush opened federal lands to timber and mining interests at giveaway fees. He doubled the already immense military spending. He more than doubled the national debt for the benefit of rich creditors and at great cost to public programs and taxpayers.
- Bush overturned the Iraqi government, shattered Iraq's state economy, and created a multi-billion-dollar bonanza of war contracts for US corporate investors. When it was revealed that Iraq was not linked to Al Qaeda and did not harbor weapons of mass destruction, Bush covered his lies by claiming he had been misled by faulty information.

In sum, while promoting an appearance of innocent bungling, President Bush advanced his agenda with rather impressive success.[21]

US rulers pretend to an innocence they seldom attain. No less a political personage than Henry Kissinger repeatedly pleaded innocent ignorance and incompetence when confronted with the dirty role he and his cohorts played in East Timor, Indochina, Chile, Bangladesh, and elsewhere.[22] He would have us believe that the people he worked for were nincompoops, not imperial operatives.

Secrecy is another phenomenon that would—by definition—suggest the existence of hidden agendas. If policymakers have nothing to hide, why do they hide so much? An estimated 21,500 US government documents are classified every workday of the year.[23] Some of these materials eventually come to light decades later—and can still be quite revealing. Thus, an October 1970 cable to CIA operatives in Chile from Kissinger's "Track Two" group (released over thirty years later) states, "It is firm and continuing policy that [the democratically elected government of Salvador] Allende be overthrown by a coup.... We are to continue to generate maximum pressure toward this end utilizing every appropriate resource. *It is imperative that these actions be implemented clandestinely and securely so that the USG* [United States Government] *and American hand be well hidden"* [italics added].[24] If the public utterances of policymakers represent their real intentions, if they have no hidden agendas, then why do they find it necessary to hide their actions not only from the US public but sometimes even from their own staffs?[25]

Sometimes outcomes are explained away as the innocent result of organizational inertia. With this mode of analysis there is no intentional human application to speak of. Interventions are said to occur because a national security agency wants to prove its usefulness or is simply carried along on its own organizational momentum, as supposedly happened with the CIA and Pentagon intervention in the Bay of Pigs invasion of Cuba. To be sure, organizational interests do come into play, but to see them as the predominant force behind policies is like claiming that the horses are the cause of the horse race.

Anything Except Moneyed Interests

Some people might complain that the analysis presented herein is simplistic and insufficiently nuanced because it ascribes everything to purely economic and class motives while ignoring other variables like geopolitics, culture, ethnicity, nationalism, ideology, morality, and leadership psychology. But I do not ascribe everything to purely economic interests. To focus on powerful corporate class interests that are usually ignored is not to claim that nothing else is to be considered as acting upon events. I do not argue that the struggle to maintain capitalist global hegemony explains everything about world politics or even everything about US foreign policy. However, it does explain quite a lot—so it is time we become aware of it and be willing to speak its name.

International capitalism is not the only consideration but it is the most crucial one. We do not have to stay transfixed upon it, but we ought to give some consideration to the role played by moneyed protagonists in international politics. If policymakers give such serious consideration to the global interests of their super rich financial class, might not we also?

It is a passion among certain academics to claim authorship to nuanced perceptions, that is, perceptions of many complexities. These complexities often turn out to be just so much polished evasion, whose primary function is to deny consideration of powerful economic factors. If such opinion makers really want to portray political life in all its manifold complexities, then we might expect that they be less studiously reticent about the immense realities of economic imperialism. They might consider how the process of global capitalist domination assumes many dimensions, including the economic realm as well as the political, military, and cultural.

The existence of other variables such as nationalism, militarism, the search for national security, and the pursuit of power and hegemonic dominance compels us neither to dismiss economic realities nor to treat these other variables as insulated from moneyed interests. Thus, to argue that US rulers intervene in one or another region not because of economic interests but for strategic reasons may sound to some like a more nuanced view, but in most cases, empirical examination shows that the desire to extend US strategic power is impelled at least in part by a desire to stabilize the area along lines that are favorable to political-economic elite interests—which is usually why the region becomes a focus of concern in the first place.

Various considerations are not mutually exclusive but work upon each other. The growth in overseas investments invites a need for military protection, just as military interventions open opportunities for overseas investment and the expansion of free market production in new parts of the world. All this, in turn, creates a need to secure bases and establish alliances with other nations. The alliances now expand the defense perimeter that must be maintained. So a particular country not only becomes an "essential" asset in the support of US defenses but must itself be defended, like any other asset.

To repeat, US leaders may have other concerns, such as advancing their nation's prestige, maintaining national security against potentially competing (capitalist and noncapitalist) nations, developing strategic military superiority, distracting the American public from domestic problems and scandals, advancing the heroic macho image of the president, and the like. But these purposes almost always dovetail with dominant capitalist interests, or certainly do not challenge those interests in any serious way. No US president, for instance, would ever think of promoting his (or her) macho image by heroically supporting the cause of socialist revolution in this or any other country.

The point is not that nations act imperialistically for purely material motives but that the ideological and psychic motives, embraced with varying degrees of sincerity by individual policymakers, unfailingly serve the systemic interests of the dominant moneyed class. In short, US political-corporate elites have long struggled to make the world safe for transnational capital accumulation; to attain control of the markets, lands, natural resources, and cheap labor of all countries; and to prevent the emergence of revolutionary socialist, populist, or even nationalist régimes that refuse to submit to this arrangement.

To achieve global hegemony, a global military machine is essential. The goal is to create a world populated by vassals (known also as "client states") and compliant populations completely open to transnational corporate penetration, on terms that are completely favorable to the transnationals. It is not too much to conclude that such a policy is produced not by dumb coincidence but by conscious effort and deliberate design.

5

How Moneyed Interests Create Poor Nations

THERE IS A "MYSTERY" WE MUST EXPLAIN. How is it that as transnational corporate investments and trade with poor countries—and international aid and loans to these same countries—have all increased dramatically over the past half century, so has world poverty? The number of people living in poverty is growing at a faster rate than the world's population. In other words, poverty is spreading among the many even as wealth accumulates among the few. As the global empire grows stronger, the world's working populations grow larger but poorer. What do we make of this?

"Only Themselves to Blame"

Many years ago, when I attended grade school in New York City, my teacher explained to us why people in far-off places like Africa, Asia, and Latin America (what soon became known as the Third World) lived in extreme poverty. They were poor, she said, because there was something wrong with them and their situations. They resided in hot climates that made it difficult to work industriously and caused them to be slow and lazy. Furthermore, they were in the habit of having too many children. To make matters worse, they were not very adept; they were culturally backward. Finally, she pointed out that their lands were poor, lacking in natural resources. Given all this, there was not much hope for them unless America came along and introduced them to more uplifting ways.

This view was not my grade-school teacher's personal creation. She was enunciating what was the conventional wisdom of that day. Being but a youngster, I never thought to draw a parallel between what was said about the presumed deficiencies of Third World peoples and what was said about impoverished people in America itself, including my own family. We working poor were—and still are—seen as the authors of our own plight, "culturally backward," "lazy," "having too many children," and just not at the top of our game. Same old story.

This too is the opinion about the poor held by many affluent people throughout the Third World itself—if not throughout the entire world. I once saw a documentary in which a group of prosperous, well-dressed, well-fed Paraguayans were lounging on a luxurious veranda, denouncing the deficiencies of Paraguay's indigent. One of them finally said, quite emphatically, "The poor need education." I immediately took heart at this comment. Here at last, someone was showing some understanding of what the penniless faced in a country where education was usually out of their reach. But I completely misread the sentiment. The man continued in a most emphatic key: "They need education in *how to be human beings*! They are *animals* who don't know how to *live like human beings*!" The others in the group readily concurred.

Only years later through my own independent study did I discover that every one of the explanations given about world poverty was false. True, the climate and topography of some parts of the Third World could be forbidding. But even in very dense jungles and frozen arctic regions, people applied themselves resourcefully in order to survive. In any case, they certainly were not lazy; they often worked just as hard or harder than people in more temperate climes.

Nor did they have so many more children than the rest of us. The population density of much of the Third World, especially in those days, was less than in places like the Netherlands, Japan, or England or even parts of the northeast United States. Nor were the denizens of Africa, Asia, and Latin America "culturally backward" (whatever that might mean). From ancient eras to more recent centuries, they had produced magnificent civilizations capable of impressive feats in architecture, horticulture, irrigation, arts, crafts, medicines, public hygiene, and the like, superior in many respects to what was found among the ill-washed, priest-ridden, diseased populations of European Christendom.

Quite frequently it was contact with the western colonizers that brought poverty and disaster to the indigenous populations of Africa, Latin America, and elsewhere. Once their farmlands and crops were stolen, their resources plundered, their herds slaughtered, their townships destroyed, and their peoples enslaved, deep poverty was the inescapable outcome, leaving them to be denounced as lazy, backward, and stupid. In fact, they were not underdeveloped but overexploited. Their development was never allowed to proceed in peace and self-direction.[1]

For all its own maldevelopment, illiteracy, class oppression, and violence, Europe did enjoy one telling advantage in the world, in the realm of *weaponry*. As I pointed out in an earlier work, "Muskets and cannons, Gatling guns and gunboats, and today missiles, helicopter gunships, and fighter bombers have been the deciding factors when West meets East and North meets South. Superior firepower, not superior culture, has brought the Europeans and Euro–North Americans to positions of supremacy that today are still maintained by force, though not by force alone."[2]

Wiping Out the Locals

Why are these various peoples and "failed nations" still so poor today and becoming ever poorer? What is wrong with them? Over the past half century or more, western transnational corporations and banks have invested heavily in the Third World. The transnationals are attracted by the rich natural resources, the high return that comes from low-paid labor, and the nearly complete absence of anything that cuts into profits, such as taxes, environmental regulations, worker benefits, and occupational safety codes. The US government has subsidized this flight of capital by granting tax concessions to corporations for their overseas investments, and even paying some of their relocation expenses—much to the outrage of workers here at home who see their jobs being exported.

American agribusiness cartels, heavily subsidized by US taxpayers, dump surplus products in other countries at below cost to undersell local producers. As Christopher Cook describes it, they expropriate the best land in these countries for cash-crop exports, usually monoculture crops requiring large amounts of pesticides, leaving less and less acreage for the hundreds of varieties of organically grown foods that feed local populations and sustain the local economy.[3]

Haiti is a prime example of this displacement of productive local populations. Decades of US farm imports pouring into Haiti—heavily subsidized by the US government and therefore easily sold at lower prices than local agrarian commodities—wiped out about three million small farmers, created more debt and hunger, and seriously damaged Haiti's ability to be self-sufficient.

In 2010 Bill Clinton publicly apologized for championing policies that totally destroyed Haiti's rice production. In the mid-1990s then-president Clinton encouraged Haiti to drastically cut tariffs on imported US rice. US rice growers received a federal refund of 72 cents on every dollar they expended to produce rice. Without tariff protections, the Haitian rice farmer was easily underpriced and put out of business by the heavily subsidized agribusiness growers in America. Haiti was not the only victim of this arrangement. In one year, US corporate rice production was subsidized by US taxpayers almost $1.3 billion. The rice shipped from the United States for sale in Honduras and several African countries was sold at 40 percent *below* production costs, causing 92 percent of Honduran rice farmers to lose their livelihoods.[4]

It was presumed, Clinton explained, that the displaced Haitian farmers would find new livelihoods by turning their efforts toward industrial development, though no specific full-scale program of industrialization was forthcoming. "It has not worked. It was a mistake," he concluded.[5]

It actually was less a "mistake" and more a policy of opportunistic design, fitting nicely with the export interests of US corporate agribusiness. Clinton's free trade policies toward Haiti, writes Kevin Edmunds, "deliberately reconfigured the country to fit into the new global division of labor, turning relatively self-sufficient farmers into low-wage workers in assembly plants." Despite his belated mea culpa, ex-president Clinton and his big investor friends ignored the practical ideas to restore self-sufficiency put forward by Haitian popular organizations. Instead they continued to bolster export-oriented agri-business cash-crops like coffee, mangos, and avocados.[6]

Instances of local industries and farming being wiped out by highly subsidized US products can be found across the globe from the Philippines to Honduras, from Mexico to Africa. In 2002 alone the US government allotted $3.7 billion in subsidies to its cotton agribusiness, which was then able to undersell African cotton producers. Countries like Benin, Burkina Faso, Chad, Togo, Kenya, and Mali lost up to $400 million in potential export revenue as a result.[7]

By displacing people from their lands and robbing them of their self-sufficiency, corporations create labor markets overcrowded with desperate populations forced into shanty towns to toil for poverty wages (when they can get work), often in violation of the country's own minimum wage laws. In various Third World countries, workers are paid pennies per hour by corporate giants such as Nike, Disney, Walmart, and J.C. Penney.[8]

The United States was one of the few nations that refused to sign an international convention for the abolition of child labor and forced labor. The convention protested the child labor practices of US corporations throughout the Third World and within the United States itself, where child workers suffer high rates of injuries and fatalities and are often paid well below the minimum wage. Across the entire planet an estimated 158 million children aged five to fourteen are engaged in child labor.[9]

Shoes made by Indonesian children working twelve-hour days for 13 cents an hour cost less than $5 to be made but still sell for $150 or more in the United States. The savings that big business reaps from cheap labor abroad are not passed on in lower prices to their customers at home. Corporations do not outsource to far-off regions so that US consumers can save money. They outsource in order to increase their margin of profit.

Phony Aid

Working hand in hand with these transnational investments are the *foreign aid* programs. US aid to other countries subsidizes construction of the infrastructure needed by corporations: ports, highways, and refineries. Aid given to Third World governments comes with strings attached. It often must be spent on US products. The recipient nation is required to give first preference to US companies, relying less on home-produced commodities in favor of imported ones, thereby creating more dependency and debt and leaving these countries less able to feed themselves.[10]

A good chunk of US aid money never sees the light of day, going directly into the personal coffers of sticky-fingered officials in the recipient countries. The very ease by which these officials are bought off makes them the favored choices of the powerful investor interests. Better to have readily cooperative and corrupt leaders who help themselves rather than dedicated incorruptible leaders who mobilize popular sentiment to resist foreign takeovers.

Aid (of a sort) also comes from other sources. In 1944 the United Nations created the World Bank and the International Monetary Fund. Voting power in both organizations is determined by a country's financial contribution. As the largest "donor," the United States has a dominant voice, followed by Germany, Japan, France, and Great Britain. Though it has 186 countries as members, the IMF operates in secrecy with a select group of bankers and finance-ministry staffs drawn mostly from the rich nations.

The World Bank and IMF are supposed to assist nations in their development. What actually happens is another story. The World Bank will lend money to this or that country to finance a huge dam project that displaces thousands of families while providing cheap irrigation for export agriculture and cheap power for a private company.[11] Or a poor country may borrow from the World Bank to build up some aspect of its economy. Should it be unable to pay back the heavy interest because of declining export sales or some other reason, it must borrow again, this time from the IMF. But the IMF imposes a "structural adjustment program" (SAP), requiring debtor countries to grant tax breaks to the transnational corporations, reduce local wages, and make no attempt to protect native enterprises from foreign imports and foreign takeovers.

In accordance with SAP rulings, the debtor nations are pressured to privatize their economies, selling at scandalously low prices their state-owned mines, railroads, and utilities to transnational corporations. They are forced to open their forests to clear-cutting and their lands to strip mining, without regard to the ecological damage done. The debtor nations also must reduce or eliminate subsidies for health, education, transportation, and food, spending less on public needs in order to have more money to meet debt payments. So it is that throughout the Third World, real wages have declined, and national debts have soared to the point at which debt payments absorb almost all of the poorer countries' export earnings—leaving the debtor country even less able to provide for the minimal needs of its population.[12]

Here then we have explained a "mystery." (It is, of course, no mystery at all if you don't adhere to trickle-down mystification.) Why has poverty deepened while foreign aid, loans, and investments have grown? Answer: loans, investments, and most forms of aid are not designed to fight poverty but to augment the wealth of transnational investors at the expense of local populations. There is no trickle down, only a siphoning up from those who labor to those who accumulate.

It Works Well for Somebody

In their perpetual confusion, some liberal critics conclude that foreign aid and IMF and World Bank SAPs "do not work" because the end result is *less* self-sufficiency and more poverty for the recipient nations. Why then do the rich member states continue to fund the IMF and World Bank? Are their leaders just not as intelligent as the liberal critics who keep pointing out to them that their "failed" policies are having the opposite effect?

In fact, it is the critics who are stupid, not the western leaders and investors who enjoy such immense wealth and success and own so much of the world. They pursue their aid and foreign loan programs because such programs *do* work. The question is, work for whom? *Cui bono?* (Who benefits?)

The function of overseas investments, loans, and aid is not to uplift the masses in other countries. (There's no profit in that.) It is to advance the imperial interests of the global capital accumulators, to help them take over the lands and local economies of Third World peoples, monopolize their markets, depress their wages, indenture their labor with enormous debts, privatize their public service sector, and prevent these nations from emerging as trade competitors by depriving them of normal development. In these respects, investments, foreign loans, and structural adjustment programs work very well indeed.

The real mystery is: why do some commentators find such an analysis so improbable? Why do they dismiss it as a "conspiracy theory"? Why are they skeptical that US rulers knowingly and deliberately pursue policies in the Third World (suppress wages, roll back environmental protections, diminish the public sector, cut back human services) designed to benefit the global corporate interests? These are the same policies that the same US rulers pursue on behalf of the same moneyed interests right here in our own country. Why would any of these players behave so differently elsewhere?

The United Nations Research Institute for Social Development released a 2005–2006 report showing that *half the world's wealth is owned by 2 percent of the richest adults.* It is time that liberal critics stop thinking that the people who own so much of the world—and want to own it all—are "incompetent" or "misguided" or "failing to see the unintended consequences of their policies." When we think the empire builders are being stupid, we are not being very smart ourselves. They know what they are doing; they know where their interests lie—and so should we.

6

Globalization
for the Few

ALONG WITH CORPORATE INVESTMENT and US foreign aid, another
way the empire accumulates wealth and spreads poverty is by imposing international rulings misleadingly referred to as *free trade* and
globalization.

Introducing "Globalization"

The goal of the transnational corporation is to become truly transnational, poised above the sovereign power of any particular nation,
while being served by the sovereign powers of all nations. Among the
measures contrived by international business to achieve dominion over
the entire planet is *globalization*. As presented to the public, globalization is just part of a natural and inevitable expansion of trade and

economic development beneficial to all. In early times, there were only village markets; these eventually expanded into regional markets, then national ones, then international ones, and now finally global agreements that cover the entire world.

As presented to the public, globalization supposedly was going to create more jobs and prosperity by abolishing restrictive regulatory laws and by integrating nation-state economies into a more open and active trade system. In fact, these "free trade" arrangements represent a kind of global coup d'état by the giant business interests of the world.

With the North American Free Trade Agreement (NAFTA), the General Agreement on Tariffs and Trade (GATT), the General Agreement on Trade in Services (GATS), and numerous other multilateral international covenants, the transnational corporations have been elevated above the sovereign powers of nation-states.[1] These agreements endow anonymous international trade committees such as the World Trade Organization (WTO), established in 1994, with the authority to overrule any nation-state laws that are deemed a burden to the investment opportunities of transnational corporations.

These trade panels consist of "trade specialists" elected by no one and drawn from the corporate world. They meet in secret and often have investment stakes in the very issues they adjudicate, being bound by no conflict-of-interest provisions. Their function is to allow the transnational companies to do whatever they wish without any regulations placed on them by any country. Not one of GATT's 500 pages of rules and restrictions are directed against private corporations; all are against governments. Signatory governments must lower tariffs, end farm subsidies, treat foreign companies the same as domestic ones, honor all transnational corporate patent claims on natural resources, and obey the rulings of a permanent elite bureaucracy, the WTO.

Should a country refuse to change its laws when a WTO panel so dictates, the WTO can impose fines or international trade sanctions, depriving the resistant country of needed markets and materials.[2] The

WTO has ruled against laws deemed *barriers to free trade*. It has forced Japan to accept greater pesticide residues in imported food. It has kept Guatemala from outlawing deceptive advertising of baby food. It has eliminated the ban that various countries had imposed on asbestos and on fuel and emission standards for motor vehicles. And the WTO has ruled against marine-life protection laws and the ban some nations imposed on the importation of endangered-species products.

The European Union banned the importation of hormone-ridden US beef, a ruling that had overwhelming popular support throughout Europe, but a three-member WTO panel decided the ban was an *illegal restraint on trade*. The WTO decision on beef put in jeopardy a host of other food import regulations based on health concerns. The WTO overturned a portion of the US Clean Air Act banning certain additives in gasoline because it interfered with imports from foreign refineries, along with a portion of the US Endangered Species Act that forbade the import of shrimp caught with nets that failed to protect sea turtles.[3]

Privatizing Nature

What is called "free trade" is neither free nor really about trade as such. Free trade is certainly not *fair* trade. It benefits strong nations at the expense of weaker ones, and rich interests at the expense of the rest of us, circumventing what little democratic sovereignty we have been able to achieve. Free trade elevates *property rights* above every other right among the nations of the world.

There is the example of the neem tree, whose extracts contain natural pesticidal and medicinal properties. Cultivated for centuries in India, the tree attracted the attention of various pharmaceutical companies that filed monopoly patents, causing mass protests by Indian farmers. As dictated by the WTO, the big pharmaceuticals now had exclusive control over the marketing of neem tree products, a ruling that would force thousands of erstwhile independent farmers to work for the powerful pharmaceuticals on low-wage terms set by the companies.

Occasional victories are won against this kind of corporate aggrandizement, including one involving the neem tree. In 1994 the European Patent Office (EPO) granted patent rights to the US Department of Agriculture and the transnational agribusiness firm WR Grace of New York for a fungicide derived from the neem tree, which it described as "an Indian medicinal plant." Following a long struggle and after being presented with subsequent evidence of traditional use of the fungicide, the EPO revoked the patent in 2005, ruling that the patent application was an act of *biopiracy*. (This was the first time a patent was rejected on such grounds.) The ruling established that the *traditional knowledge* of farmers is a right that takes precedence over the false assertions of agribusiness firms. These corporate claimants put forth a newly invented use for the neem plant to justify their monopoly grab of a natural agrarian resource that has been in common use for generations.[4]

The war to monopolize nature continues. A trade agreement between India and the United States, the Knowledge Initiative on Agriculture (KIA), backed by Monsanto and other transnational corporate giants, allows for the takeover of India's seed sector by Monsanto and India's trade sector by Archer Daniels Midland and Cargill. This amounted to a war against millions of India's independent farmers and small businesses, and a threat to that country's food security. Farmers began organizing against this economic invasion by maintaining traditional seed banks and setting up systems of communal agrarian support. As one farmer said, "We do not buy seeds from the market because we suspect they may be contaminated with genetically engineered or terminator seeds."[5]

Another corporate invasion in India was the one launched by Walmart, whose intent was to take over India's retail sector. Walmart announced plans to open 500 stores in India, starting in 2007. But several years later the government, to its credit, still was not allowing Walmart stores and other foreign companies to sell directly to consumers.[6]

The WTO ruled that the US corporation RiceTec had the patent rights to the many varieties of basmati rice grown for centuries by India's farmers. It also ruled that a Japanese corporation had exclusive rights in the entire world to grow and produce curry powder. As these instances demonstrate, what is called "free trade" amounts to *international corporate monopoly control over nature itself.* Such developments caused Malaysian prime minister Mahathir Mohamad to observe:

We now have a situation where theft of genetic resources by western biotech TNCs [transnational corporations] enables them to make huge profits by producing patented genetic mutations of these same materials. What depths have we sunk to in the global marketplace when nature's gifts to the poor may not be protected but their modifications by the rich become exclusive property?

If the current behavior of the rich countries is anything to go by, globalization simply means the breaking down of the borders of countries so that those with the capital and the goods will be free to dominate the markets.[7]

Globalization has even targeted "water markets." Recognized everywhere as a community resource and a human right, water sources are now being privatized, sold to corporations like Monsanto that then lay exclusive claim to marketing the water as a profitable commodity, in some cases even prohibiting local residents from using barrels to collect their own rainwater. The companies claim to own the water that comes from deep within the earth and from the rivers and streams, and now from the heavens too.[8]

Free trade agreements give transnational corporations control not only of production but of consumption as well. A WTO meeting was called in May 2010 in Quebec for the purpose of changing international standards on food labeling. The goal was to abolish the labeling of genetically modified (GM) foods. The US delegation sent by the Obama administration led the fight to abolish labeling. Deprived of a warning label, the public would have no way of avoiding the consumption of GM foodstuffs. In effect, Americans and the peoples of other nations would be deprived of their democratic sovereignty, their right to take protective measures against such products. It would become illegal under international law for government agencies to inform consumers that the food being sold to them was genetically modified. As it happened, the US delegation was unable to get the pro-Monsanto proposal adopted at the 2010 meeting.[9] But future attempts to wipe out protective consumer labeling lurk on the horizon.

Free Trade vs. Public Service

Globalization means turning the clock back on reforms. Health and safety regulations can be judged as imposing an unfair burden on trade. Public services can be charged with depriving foreign corporations of market opportunities.[10] To offer one instance: under NAFTA, the US-based Ethyl Corporation sued the Canadian government for $250 million in *lost business opportunities* and *interference with trade* because Canada banned MMT, an Ethyl Corporation–produced gasoline additive found to be carcinogenic by Canadian investigators. Fearing they would lose the case, Canadian officials reluctantly lifted the ban on MMT, paid Ethyl $10 million compensation, and issued a public statement calling MMT "safe," even though they had scientific findings showing otherwise. California also banned the unhealthy additive;

this time a Canadian-based Ethyl company sued California under NAFTA for placing an unfair burden on free trade.[11]

In another case the good guys won: United Parcel Service (UPS) charged the Canadian postal service for *lost market opportunities,* which means that under NAFTA, the Canadian government would have to compensate UPS for all the business that UPS thinks it would have procured had there been no public postal service in Canada. Just about all public services could be wiped out had the judgment gone as UPS wanted. The Canadian postal workers union challenged the case, arguing that the agreement violated the Canadian Constitution. The NAFTA tribunal decided on behalf of the Canadian postal service in a complicatedly argued decision. The positive effect of the decision was to free other Canadian public-service initiatives that were being held in abeyance out of fear of being charged with interfering with free trade.[12] But potential difficulties in expanding or maintaining public services continue as long as free trade agreements rule the roost.

Spreading Poverty

Agreements like GATT and NAFTA have hastened the corporate takeover of local markets in various countries, squeezing out smaller businesses and worker collectives. Under NAFTA, better-paying US jobs were lost as US firms contracted out to the cheaper Mexican labor market. In its first few years over 600,000 jobs in the United States were eliminated under NAFTA. New jobs created in that period were mostly in the lower-paying sector of the US economy. Meanwhile, Mexico was flooded with cheap, high-tech, mass-produced corn and dairy products from giant American agribusiness firms (themselves heavily subsidized by the US government), driving small Mexican farmers and distributors into bankruptcy and displacing large numbers of poor peasants and small businesses. With the advent of NAFTA, the incomes of poor Mexicans was halved, poverty spread from 30 percent to at least 50 percent of the population, and Mexican sweatshop profits skyrocketed.[13]

Under NAFTA, wages have fallen in the United States, Mexico, and Canada, and union membership has shrunk dramatically. Canada has lost tens of thousands of well-paying jobs. Companies now can more easily move operations across borders to cheaper labor markets, a threat that has further undermined union organizing and deterred wage demands.[14]

African nations like Ghana, Uganda, and Mali found that their gross domestic product (GDP) declined sharply with the advent of free trade. Contrary to the promises of prosperity put forth by free trade advocates, when poor countries phase out tariff protections, import quotas, and import duties designed to protect their local industries, "imports climb sharply and local producers are priced out of the market by cheaper, often subsidized Western goods. This also depresses prices."[15]

North Americans are told that to remain competitive in this newly globalized world marketplace, they must increase their output while reducing their labor costs; in other words, work harder for less pay in what has been called a *race to the bottom*. This is happening. The work-week lengthened by as much as 20 percent (from forty hours to forty-six and even forty-eight hours) and real wages flattened or declined during the reign of George W. Bush, continuing into the Barack Obama era.

During the deep recession ushered in by the financial crises of 2008, some of the millions of unemployed eventually were able to gain reentry into the US workforce. But many of the new jobs were part-time, of limited duration, lower pay, and lacking in benefits. Bosses had their pick of workers willing to accept less secure positions. Many have been rehired as "self-employed contract workers," often doing the same work they once did as full-time employees, only now for a limited duration and for lower pay and no benefits. By 2005 almost one-third of the workforce consisted of these so-called contingent workers. By the end of the decade the number was estimated at closer to 40 percent.[16]

In sum, globalization diminishes the living standards of working people not only in the Third World but in the major industrial countries as well. As represented by the free trade agreements, globalization is not an inevitable "natural" development. The trade agreements have been consciously planned by big business and its government minions over a period of years in pursuit of a totally deregulated world economy that *undermines all democratic checks on business practices.* The people of any one province, state, or nation are now finding it increasingly difficult to get their governments to impose protective regulations or develop new forms of public-sector production out of fear of being overruled by some self-appointed international free trade panel.[17]

Bending the Rules

Usually it is large nations demanding that poorer, smaller ones relinquish the protections and subsidies they provide for their local producers. But occasionally things take a different turn. In late 2006 Canada launched a dispute at the World Trade Organization over the use of *trade-distorting* agricultural subsidies by the United States, specifically the enormous sums dished out by the US government to agribusiness, enabling US farm corporations to sell commodities abroad at prices lower than what the farmers in other countries can offer, thereby creating an unfair advantage in agrarian exports. The case also challenged the entire multibillion-dollar structure of US agricultural subsidies. A report by Oxfam International revealed that at least thirty-eight Third World countries were suffering severely as a result of trade-distorting subsidies by both the United States and the European Union.[18]

The US government attempted to insert a special clause into trade negotiations that would place its illegal use of farm subsidies above challenge by WTO member countries and make the subsidies immune from adjudication by the WTO. In 2009 the WTO ruled that "massive government subsidies for large-scale cotton growers in the United States are unfair and hurt farmers in poor countries." An Oxfam study found that a complete removal of US cotton subsidies would lift the world price of cotton by 6 to 14 percent, resulting in better markets and increased income for many poor West African cotton-growing households. But US rulers continued as before, refusing to abide by the WTO ruling to scrap its subsidies.[19] The empire always places itself above the strictures it imposes on others.

WTO aside, what is seldom remarked upon is that NAFTA and GATT are in violation of the US Constitution, the preamble of which makes clear that sovereign power rests with the people: "We the People of the United States ... do ordain and establish this Constitution for the United States of America." Article I, Section 1 of the Constitution notes that all legislative powers shall be vested in the US Congress. Article I, Section 7 gives the president (not some trade council) the power to veto a law, subject to being overridden by a two-thirds vote in Congress. And Article III gives adjudication and review powers to federal courts, not to self-appointed trade tribunals. The Ninth and Tenth Amendments to the Constitution declare that all rights and powers not explicitly delegated to the federal government are reserved to the people and the states. In a word, there is nothing in the entire Constitution that allows—and much that disallows—an international trade panel to exercise supreme review powers undermining the constitutionally mandated decisions of the legislative, executive, and judicial branches.

True, Article VII says that the Constitution, federal laws, and *treaties* "shall be the supreme Law of the land," but this was not intended to include treaties that overrode the sovereign democratic power of the people and their representatives. In any case, strictly speaking, the trade agreements are not treaties. NAFTA and GATT were called "agreements" instead of treaties, a semantic ploy that enabled President Clinton to bypass the two-thirds treaty ratification vote in the Senate and avoid any treaty amendment process. The World Trade Organization was approved by a lame-duck session of Congress held after the 1994 elections. No lawmaker running in that election uttered a word to voters about putting the US government under a perpetual obligation to international trade rulings.

What is being undermined is not only a lot of good laws dealing with environment, public services, labor standards, and consumer protection but also the very right to legislate such laws. Our *democratic sovereignty* itself is being surrendered to a secretive plutocratic trade organization that presumes to exercise a power greater than that of the people and their courts and legislatures.

"Free trade" is designed to leave the world's economic (and ecological) destiny to the tender mercy of bankers and transnational corporations. The globalization it promotes is a logical extension of imperialism, a victory of empire over republic, a victory of international finance capital over local productivity and nation-state democracy (such as it is).

Militant protests against free trade have taken place in over forty nations, from Britain and France to Thailand and India. In 2000–2001 alone, there were demonstrations in Seattle, Sydney, Prague, Genoa, Washington, D.C., and various other locales, causing several multilateral trade agreements to be stalled or voted down. Poorer nations were catching wise to the free trade scams and refusing to sign away what shreds of sovereignty they still had.

Some Confused Marxists

The discussion of globalization by some prominent Marxists (but not all) has oddly focused on the question of whether the new "internationalization" of capital will undermine national sovereignty and the nation-state. Invariably these observers (for instance, Ellen Wood and William Taab in *Monthly Review;* Ian Jasper and Morris Zeitlin in *Nature, Society, and Thought*; and Erwin Marquit in *Political Affairs*) conclude that the nation-state still plays a key role in capitalist imperialism, that capital—while global in its scope—is not international but bound to particular nations, and that "globalization" is little more than another name for overseas capital investment.

They repeatedly remind us that Karl Marx already had described globalization, this process of international financial expansion, as early as 1848, when he and Friedrich Engels in the *Communist Manifesto* wrote about how capitalism moves into all corners of the world, refashioning all things into its own image. Therefore, there is no cause for the present uproar. Globalization, these Marxists conclude, is not a new development but a long-standing one that Marxist theory uncovered long ago. Nor is there any reason to fear, they assure us, that the nation-state will disappear from history because of the globalization of trade and production.

The problem with this position is that it misses the whole central point of the current struggle. It is not *national* sovereignty that is at stake, it is *democratic* sovereignty. People all over the world have taken to the streets to protest free trade agreements not out of concern for their flag but for their democratic rights, their ability to defend themselves from the preemptive expropriations of an internationalized monopoly capital. Among them are farmers, workers, students, and intellectuals, including many Marxists who see things more clearly than the aforementioned.

As used today, the term *globalization* refers to a new stage of international expropriation, designed not to put an end to the nation-state but to undermine whatever democratic right exists to protect the social wage and restrain the power of transnational corporations.

The free trade agreements potentially can override all statutes and regulations that restrict private capital in any way. Carried to full realization, this means the end of whatever imperfect democratic protections people have been able to muster after generations of struggle. Under the free trade agreements, any and all public services can be ruled out of existence because they cause "lost market opportunities" for private capital. So too, public hospitals can be charged with taking away markets from foreign-owned private hospitals; and public water supply systems, public schools, public housing, and public transportation are guilty of depriving their private counterparts in other countries of market opportunities, likewise public health insurance, public mail delivery, and public auto insurance systems. Laws that try to protect the environment or labor standards or consumer health already have been overturned for "creating barriers to free trade."

But let it be repeated: what also is overthrown is the *right* to have such laws. This is the most important point of all and the one most frequently overlooked by persons from across the political spectrum. Under the free trade accords, corporate investment rights have been upraised to imperial supremacy, able to take precedent over all other rights, including the right to a clean, livable environment, the right to affordable public services, and the right to any morsel of political-economic democracy. *Under the banner of "free trade," corporate property rights are elevated above all democratic rights.*

Globalization has been used to stifle the voice of working people and their ability to develop a public sector that serves their interests. Even free speech is being undermined by free trade agreements as when *product disparagement* (public criticism of the safety or quality of a product) is treated as an interference with international trade. And even nature itself is being privatized by transnational capital, as corporations buy up patents to monopolize the world's natural food supply. What we have is an international coup d'état by big capital over the peoples of the world.

Another form of laissez-faire supremacy not mentioned so far (and given relatively slight attention by Marxists) is the European Union (EU). It is a 27-state confederation in which "free movement" of goods, services, capital, and labor are promoted, and no EU member state is allowed to protect local producers from the competition of a more powerful transnational company situated in another member state. As there are substantial income disparities between member states, "free movement," as Anthony Coughlin points out, leads to wider inequalities, with "high cost capital and businesses tending to move from Western to Eastern Europe and low cost labor moving from Eastern Europe westward."[20]

In sum, the fight against free trade is a fight for the right to political-economic democracy, public services, and a social wage, the right not to be completely at the mercy of big capital. It is a new and drastic phase of the class struggle that some Marxists—so immersed in classical theory and so ill-informed about present-day public policy— seem to have missed. The free trade accords benefit the rich nations over poor ones and the rich classes within all nations at the expense of ordinary citizens. It is the new imperial specter that haunts the world.

7

Free Market Servitude

AROUND THE WORLD THE EMPIRE BUILDERS and plutocrats extend their reach, expropriating land, labor, resources, and markets, gathering still more and more riches unto themselves. Marinating in their immense wealth, the laissez-faire disciples tirelessly sing hosannas to the empire's prime mythic creation, the free market, that magical blend of individual greed and supposedly collective benefit. In this chapter we investigate in some detail the blessings of the free market as bestowed upon the victimized populations of several countries.

Impunity for the Oligarchs

Here is an incident that occurred in Honduras. It demonstrates how the power distributions of a free market society can act with brutal effect on existing social relations.

Not long ago the veteran author and journalist John Gerassi wrote to me: "Honduras is run by a tight little oligarchy which includes its congress and supreme court." The oligarchs kill those who dare to challenge their privileged exploitation. They even kill just to demonstrate their absolutist power. "When I visited the farm of such an oligarch, while researching my book *The Great Fear in Latin America*," Gerassi goes on, "I asked him why he paid his peons so little. 'They're pigs,' he answered, 'the only thing they respect is power. They have to know that I have life and death power over them. Only then will they work.' Stupidly, I asked: 'Do they know that?' He laughed, called over one of the peons, took out his pistol and shot him in the head. When I reported this killing to the Tegucigalpa chief of police, he quipped: 'Yes, but he owns that *estancia* [farmland].'"[1]

The investigative writer Andre Vltchek informs me that similar atrocities have happened in the Philippines, Indonesia, and elsewhere in Southeast Asia, a region in which he has spent many years. "In Indonesia, the owner of a former Hilton Hotel shot to death (in public) a waiter simply because the owner's friend complained that the service was bad. After one year in prison, the murderer is once again free."[2]

In the free market society of a Third World country like Honduras or Indonesia, the peon is little more than a slave. His or her life is of no value apart from its capacity to create value for the owner through hard work at a subsistence wage. In the murderous vignette Gerassi described, we see how the landlord's immense economic power translates into political and moral *impunity*. Conversely, the peon's economic *powerlessness* translates into political impotence, the inability to make a minimal legal claim to one's labor and even to one's own life.

That is what the free market is about: the freedom of plutocrats to do whatever they want to those in economic servitude whose lives have become expendable and easily replaceable.

Free Market Pauperism

Frequently we hear that the free market is the path to material prosperity and the laissez-faire paradise. All an impoverished nation need do is put its public services and properties (utilities, media, farmlands, transportation systems, hospitals, banks, factories) up for sale to rich investors. Along with this *privatization* of social capital, the destitute country should pursue a policy of *deregulation*, that is, "liberate" the entire private economy from the irksome constraints of government regulation, reducing government functions to a bare minimum. To make its economy truly laissez-faire, the country also must eliminate tariff protections and open its economy and natural resources to foreign investors and exporters.

This completely privatized and unprotected neoliberal economic model supposedly benefits all nations in all circumstances. "This gospel," Gregory Elich observes, "is preached by the US and Western European nations and enforced through international financial institutions such as the International Monetary Fund, World Bank and World Trade Organization."[3] Their dazzling prognostications bear no resemblance to the actual experiences endured by working people around the world.

Consider what happened to Ghana when the free marketeers moved in on that West African nation. In accordance with agreements it had signed with the IMF and World Bank, Ghana enacted structural adjustment programs, consisting of cutbacks in government supports and services. "Subsidies to farmers were ended and the state-run seed company was closed down," Elich reports. "State-provided tractor services and land clearing operations were halted. Government programs that actively supported farmers were ended. Import tariffs were dramatically reduced and in many cases eliminated altogether. This led to a flood of cheap imports from abroad." Local farmers were forced into a highly unequal trade war not of their choosing, unable to compete against imports from heavily subsidized, large-scale western agribusiness.[4] Deeply in debt to the IMF and World Bank, Third World governments are prohibited from spending on domestic subsidies and required to use their funds to meet IMF/World Bank payments.

In Ghana this one-sided arrangement has succeeded in driving many farmers into severest hardship. For example, the heavily subsidized tomato paste imports into Ghana from the United States and Western Europe have increased by more than five times in one decade and have driven out local tomato farming and processing plants. The local cannery in one farmer's area, which had "made things easier for us," was now closed. Being a state-run firm, it was no longer allowed to operate without a private buyer. "Selling our tomatoes is a game of chance," the farmer said. "It's heartbreaking to stand here and watch the fruit go rotten."[5]

"Poultry imports into Ghana have increased so much," reports Elich, "that many domestic farms are having to slaughter thousands of chickens a week due to market glut. Hatcheries are operating at under half their capacity." In Senegal over a six-year period, poultry imports increased 33 times over, driving 40 percent of poultry farmers out of business. In Cameroon, a threefold increase in poultry imports eventually put 92 percent of poultry farmers out of business.[6] Similar stories can be told about poultry farmers in Central America and elsewhere, undersold and driven out by the influx of frozen chemical-ridden chickens from heavily subsidized US factory farms.

In Mozambique, Senegal, and other parts of Africa, local farm and factory production was just about completely wiped out by corporate imports. In Côte d'Ivoire, "the ten rice mills that had been built by the state-owned rice company were privatized. Two years later, not one remained in business. Inevitably, the privatization drive closed down the rice company."[7] The same held true for state-owned seed farms.

Over the past two decades, Africa lost approximately $272 billion because of the corporate takeover of domestic food production. "That money did not vanish," Elich notes. "It is being transferred to wealthy pockets in the developed nations."[8] Free trade means privatization for the few and privation for the many.

The Global Sweatshop

Elich reports that in recent years, "the reign of free market ideology has brought a disturbing rise in sweatshop manufacturing, with conditions reminiscent of the worst of the nineteenth century." In sweatshops that act as suppliers to big corporations like Walmart, Nike, and Adidas, employment "is akin to imprisonment. The Alejandro Apparel plant in Honduras is representative of sweatshops throughout the Third World, with its barbed-wire fence, locked gates and armed security guards.... [T]he firm is exempt from all taxes, import and export duties and tariffs."[9]

Workers put in ten- and twelve-hour shifts, nonstop, for pennies an hour. In some plants, employees are regularly required to work unpaid overtime to meet impossibly high production quotas. "The supervisors stand over us shouting and cursing at us to go faster," one former worker testifies. Workers spend all day toiling as fast as they can, breathing in dust particles, sweating under the factory heat, not allowed to stretch or even look to the side. "By the end of the day your whole body aches, your back, arms, shoulders, everything."[10]

Elich offers other accounts of labor conditions in the free market:

In Bangladesh, workers sew garments for Disney and Walmart, earning the princely sum of 11 to 20 cents per hour.... The pay is so abysmal that four workers must share a single shack, and one outhouse and water pump serves sixty people. Meals consist of nothing but rice, only occasionally flavored with a small amount of beans or potatoes. To manage even such a meager diet as this, workers must borrow money each week. The workweek is fourteen hours a day, seven days a week. If a worker is caught talking in the factory, he is fined a day's wages. "It is a bleak life. We have no hope," confessed one worker. Another complained, "We have no life. We can't afford to marry; we have no wife, no social life. We live just to work."[11]

At the Western Dresses factory in Dhaka, Bangladesh, a worker reports that he worked six months straight without a single day off. "My job was to sew the flaps on the back pockets of these pants. I had to sew 120 pieces an hour. It was difficult to reach. If you made any mistakes or fell behind on your goal, they beat you.... This happens very often. They hit you hard." Workers at the factory are not permitted to talk, and if they even dare to stand and stretch, their pay is cut.[12] Such are some of the less publicized features of the free market paradise. (In contrast, work conditions in communist countries such as Vietnam and China were never that horrible and have been improving in recent years.)

Destroying Self-Development

Another country over which the free market reigns supreme is Indonesia. Its public sector has been whittled down to almost nothing while its unregulated and untaxed private sector waxes ever grander. As in so many other countries, Indonesia's free market society did not arise by natural growth but by force and violence.

Under President Sukarno's earlier progressive government, Indonesia seemed to be developing a viable public sector replete with social programs, public libraries, schools, and health clinics, many of them tended by the PKI, the Indonesian Communist Party. But in 1965–1966, the Indonesian military—armed, advised, and financed by the US Pentagon and CIA—overthrew the Sukarno government and, with the help of militant Islamic groups, massacred upwards of a million people (some Indonesian generals involved in the massacres brag of as many as three million victims), including trade unionists, PKI members, ethnic Chinese, and community organizers in what amounted to the greatest political mass slaughter since the Holocaust.[13]

In some parts of the country up to 40 percent of the teachers were killed, with many others imprisoned. Reading rooms and libraries were destroyed; books were burned; film studios and theaters were shut down; intellectuals were either murdered, incarcerated, or driven into hiding. Cultural life all but disappeared. After decades of military dictatorship, Indonesia ended up with one of the most under-funded and dismal educational systems in the world.[14]

Looming over the bloodletting was General Suharto, who had served with Japanese fascist forces during World War II. For more than three decades, Suharto's régime enjoyed the support of the United States, Australia, and most of the governments of Southeast Asia and Europe, along with the international business community. The mass atrocities he perpetrated went largely unnoticed and uncriticized by the US government and mainstream media.

In 1975, Suharto launched an invasion of East Timor, causing the death of at least 100,000 people and wreaking vast destruction upon that country in an effort to prevent the East Timorese from taking an independent and revolutionary path. President Gerald Ford and Secretary of State Henry Kissinger had given Suharto the go-ahead on the invasion on 6 December 1975 and secretly provided him with the arms and logistical back-up he needed.[15]

The Indonesian occupation of East Timor continued for twenty-five blood-drenched years. "The terrorizing and plundering" of East Timor and recalcitrant provinces like Aceh and Papua "were not opposed by major Western powers as long as their companies had direct access to Indonesia's natural resources," reported Andre Vltchek, a leading authority on that region.[16]

Suharto presided over what was hailed in the western press as an Indonesian "success story," specifically the total privatization of the nation's rich natural resources, bringing great profits to foreign mining and oil companies and to Suharto himself, who amassed an estimated $35 billion by the time he died in 2008. Corruption extended to other officials and family members as well.[17]

With every encouragement from his western patrons, Suharto turned Indonesia into a supplier of raw materials and assembly-line cheap labor for multinational companies. The economy was not only privatized but thoroughly deregulated. Indonesia now has one of the "purest" free market economies in the world, much to the pleasure of US investors and policymakers.

When Life Is Unregulated—and Cheap

One tragic consequence of Indonesia's unregulated laissez-faire economy is that people live unprotected lives; many die prematurely, the society's infrastructure (such as it is) is collapsing, and poverty grows evermore severe.

"Hunger and malnutrition remain the most devastating problems facing the majority of Indonesians," festering in some form in almost every district of the country, according to one Indonesian health official. "At present, about one-half of the population is iron-deficient and one-third is at risk of iodine deficiency disorders. Vitamin A deficiency still affects around ten million children."[18]

Indonesia's state hospitals are in dire condition, reports Vltchek. Medical service is so dangerously substandard and open to corrupt practices that most Indonesians avoid hospitals and clinics.[19]

Indonesia also is beset by manmade disasters. Poorly maintained airliners disappear in flight or careen off runways. Worn ferry boats sink or break apart on the high seas. Ports are in ruinous conditions. Trains crash or are derailed on the average of one a week. Dilapidated buses regularly end up as roadside wrecks. Cheaply constructed and neglected houses collapse and kill their occupants. There are no occupational or consumer protections to speak of. It is *buyer beware* and *worker watch out.* Communities of garbage scavengers are accidentally buried alive under massive illegal foul-smelling dumps. Landslides push makeshift dwellings into ravines. Floods and tidal waves destroy unprotected villages. Life is cheap in this free market paradise. In less than three years, Indonesia lost some 200,000 people in disasters, not counting automobile accidents and military actions.[20] The country's news media report these tragic mishaps but without reference to the corrupt, unregulated laissez-faire governance that does nothing to prevent such catastrophes and much to make them happen.

Indonesia has plenty of materiel to build safe homes and communities, notes Vltchek, plenty to modernize rail lines and buses, construct walls and levies to protect against floods, and reinforce the hills around towns that are in danger of being crushed by landslides. But there is no profit in such ventures. The free market has no interest in human needs that are not backed by commercial buying power. Instead, construction goes into dozens of new shopping malls in Jakarta and mansions for corrupt officials.[21]

Public spaces that might be used for parks and playgrounds are turned into golf courses and luxury clubs for the very affluent. Indonesia's economic elites, the free market's winners, are little concerned about how the impoverished masses might fare. They themselves reside in grand comfort, served by an underpaid and obedient labor force of nannies, maids, drivers, gardeners, and cooks.[22]

Vltchek describes the misery and squalor that free market imperial power brings to the common people:

One turn [off] from the main streets and the real Jakarta exposes its wounds: filthy narrow alleys, channels clogged with garbage, makeshift stores selling unhygienic food, children running barefoot; thousands of big and small mosques, but not one decent playground for children. Garbage accumulates at every corner and polluted air penetrates throat and eyes. Little girls are offering themselves for a pittance, while boys are sniffing glue from plastic bags.

Each year, Indonesia destroys more forests than any other country in the world. Deforestation causes landslides, and as a result thousands of people die annually as their houses slide into ravines.

The train system has not been overhauled since the Dutch colonial administration (circa 1942). Trains are regularly derailed. Passengers trying to save money on fares occasionally fall to their death through the rusty roofs on which they are traveling. No Indonesian city has an acceptable public transportation system. Some, including Bandung (with three million people), are served only by a few dilapidated buses and private minivans.[23]

Indonesian elites retain fond memories of Suharto. After destroying Sukarno's government and slaughtering the egalitarian popular movement in 1965–1966, Suharto imposed a corrupt reactionary rule, backed by an Indonesian military that was—and still is—in service to the US empire and its transnational corporate clients. He claimed he was saving the country while sacrificing it on the altar of laissez-faire plunder. "Since 1965," concludes Vltchek, "we have been told that oppression is democracy, that poverty is development, that censorship is freedom of expression, that a collapsing nation is not collapsing at all, and that everything is forgiven and the nation is grateful to Suharto—the departing king of Java who saved capitalism, the nation, and this entire part of the world."[24]

Another Free Market Disaster

In Chapter 4 we observed how the free market, with its privatization and deregulation, inflicted poverty and hardship on the former communist nations of Eastern Europe and the Soviet Union. Here we might give attention to Kyrgyzstan. This Central Asian former Soviet republic offers one of the best examples of how free market capitalism betrays the needs of the people. Kyrgyzstan's acceptance into the WTO came at a painful price; it had to privatize and deregulate its economy. A USAID report to the US Congress cheered this process, claiming that "Kyrgyzstan's major achievement" has been to establish the "framework for a market economy. Foreign investment is strongly encouraged and the country's privatization is regarded as among the most ambitious [most thorough] of the former Soviet republics."[25]

Almost all government-owned enterprises in Kyrgyzstan have been transferred to private ownership. The country's economy, which had been one of the best performing in Central Asia during the communist era, slowed down and actually began to contract. Its debt ballooned, consuming an ever-larger portion of the public budget. Deteriorating conditions within the country created increasingly inequitable and harsh social relations. Kyrgyzstan was transformed into a free market system that has worked supremely well for a few super rich oligarchs while wreaking havoc on the bulk of the population.

- WTO-mandated budget cuts have diminished government resources and left next to nothing for human services, causing widespread hardship among the working class population.
- Since abandoning a planned economy, Kyrgyzstan has experienced a dramatic 75 percent decline in its GDP and a notable increase in government corruption and cost of living, including a steep rise in fuel, water, and gas charges.

- Factories and state farms collapsed with the disappearance of their traditional markets in the former Soviet Union, causing further deterioration in living standards for the agrarian sector and a substantial drop in agricultural production.
- The World Health Organization reports a severely declining life expectancy since the Soviet days. A Kyrgyz population that once received free medical service now is facing rapidly escalating health costs, causing many to completely forsake medical care.
- Exports of gold, mercury, and electricity have grown, but domestically produced Kyrgyz goods are being replaced with foreign imports.
- The capitalist economy also brought a dramatic increase in organized crime dealing mainly with the smuggling of drugs from Afghanistan via Tajikistan on their way to Russia and beyond.
- The use of gas-consuming vehicles has grown in Kyrgyzstan and, coupled with increasing deforestation, has caused a marked deterioration in the country's wildlife and air quality.[26]

The free market, we are told, breeds democracy and prosperity. In fact, it brought neither democracy nor prosperity to Kyrgyzstan. Along with the economic hardships came rigged elections, police killings, riots, government harassment of dissenters, rampant corruption, national uprisings with demonstrators occupying official buildings and state-run TV stations, and bloody reprisals by security forces. Kyrgyzstan was listed by the New York Committee to Protect Journalists as one of the most difficult and dangerous places for journalists to work. By 2010, the country was being torn apart by suddenly arising interethnic conflicts among groups that had lived together in peace for decades during the Soviet era.[27]

Kyrgyzstan has become a target for repressive imperial forces because of its rich water reserves, its proximity to China, Russia, and

Afghanistan, and the need to secure the large US military base on its territory. The country may end up as another target in Washington's "anti-terror" global counterinsurgency, subjected to external threat and internal destabilization until such time as it is reduced to being a perfectly obedient satellite thoroughly paralyzed by imperial subversion and free market poverty.[28]

When next you hear individuals singing praises to the free market, remind them that the market is free only for the global empire's moneyed patrons.

8

Target Cuba

CUBA IS ONE OF THE FEW COUNTRIES that has managed to resist—at great cost—the US counterrevolutionary juggernaut. For over a half century the island nation has been subjected to an array of hostile actions designed to undermine its economy and government. The empire justifies its aggression with a familiar mantra: Cuba is a communist régime, a threat to our freedom and an oppression to its own people; therefore we must strive for régime change, of a kind we have imposed on many other countries. Much of the American public swallows this line. We might want to question it.

The "Enemy Offshore"

During the administration of George W. Bush, relations between Washington and Havana went from bad to worse. Restrictions on trade and travel became tighter than ever. Antigovernment agitation within Cuba was financed and directed by the US Interests Section in Havana. Most ominously of all, in early 2003 US pundits began talking openly about invading Cuba—a discussion that was put on hold only after the invasion of Iraq proved so daunting and costly.

Under the Barack Obama administration in 2009, relations with Havana showed limited improvement. Some travel restrictions against Cuban artists and intellectuals were lightened but the trade embargo remained in place. Regardless of political party, US rulers continued to treat Cuba as an antagonist. Why so?

In the early days of 1959, the Cuban people, led by Fidel Castro and his guerrilla forces, overthrew the US-supported right-wing dictatorship of General Fulgencio Batista. Some five months after taking power, the revolutionary government promulgated an agrarian reform calling for state appropriation of large private landholdings. Under this new law, US sugar corporations eventually lost about 1.6 million acres of choice land and many millions of dollars in future cash-crop exports. The following year, President Dwight Eisenhower, citing Havana's "hostility" toward the United States, cut Cuba's share of the American sugar market by about 95 percent, in effect imposing a total boycott on Cuban sugar. (The only thing saving Havana from complete economic disaster at that point was the Soviet Union's willingness to buy Cuban sugar at top market prices.) A few months later, in October 1959, the Cuban government nationalized all banks and large commercial and industrial enterprises, including the many that belonged to US firms.[1]

Cuba's break away from a free market system dominated by American corporations and toward a not-for-profit socialist economy caused it to become the target of an unremitting series of US attacks that included sabotage, espionage, terrorist attacks, hijackings, assassinations, trade sanctions, travel restrictions, embargo, and outright invasion. The purpose behind this aggression was to undermine the socialist revolution and deliver Cuba safely back to the tender mercies of the free market.

In 1960 President Eisenhower issued an executive order, "Program of Covert Action against the Castro Régime," giving official approval to all kinds of illegal operations aimed at overthrowing the revolutionary government. A paramilitary force was organized that secretly entered Cuba to train terrorist groups, waging armed attacks and killing campesinos in the island's central mountains, along with a clandestine group that provided intelligence and engaged in numerous acts of sabotage.[2]

Eisenhower issued instructions that the hand of the United States should remain hidden in all this skulduggery. He made those present at the signing of the executive order swear to silence. In his memoirs Eisenhower acknowledged what happened next: "I ordered the Central Intelligence Agency to begin organizing the training of Cuban exiles in Guatemala.... Another idea was to set up an anti-Castro force inside Cuba. Some thought the United States should quarantine [i.e., blockade] the island, arguing that if the economy suddenly collapsed, the Cuban people themselves would overthrow Castro."[3]

The US policy toward Cuba was in keeping with Washington's long-standing goal of treating as a dangerous enemy any country or political movement that pursues self-development outside the global free market system. In contrast, countries deemed "friendly toward America" and "pro-West" are those that remain at the disposal of large corporate investors on terms totally favorable to the investors.

This is not what US rulers have been telling the American people. As early as July 1960, the White House charged that Cuba was "hostile" to the United States (despite Havana's repeated overtures for normal relations). The island government was a cruel dictatorship, in Eisenhower's words, "dominated by international communism."[4] Washington policymakers never explained why they were so suddenly concerned about bringing freedom and democracy to the Cuban people. In the two decades prior to the Cuban Revolution, successive administrations in Washington manifested no opposition to the brutally repressive Batista autocracy. Quite the contrary, they sent Batista military aid and carried on a vigorous business with him.

The significant but unspoken difference between Castro and Batista was that dictator Batista ruled Cuba as a perfect US satellite, wide open to the empire's capital penetration. Cuba's tourist trade, sugar and tobacco production, nickel mines, and oil refineries were owned by US corporations and a small, rich Cuban investor class. In contrast, Castro and his revolutionary movement nationalized US holdings and renovated the class structure toward a more egalitarian mode. It was this socialistic agenda that made the Cuban government so insufferable to Washington—and still does.

Aggressing Against the "Communist Aggressors"

The US modus operandi for régime change has been applied to other countries besides Cuba. It can be described as follows:

- Heap criticism on the targeted government for imprisoning the oppressors and assassins of the previous US-backed reactionary free market régime.
- Denounce the newly installed revolutionary or reformist government as "dictatorial" for failing to immediately institute Western-style electoral politics or for showing friendly relations and trading with the then-Soviet Union.
- Demonize the revolutionary leaders, labeling them as fanatical, brutal, genocidal, power hungry, and even mentally imbalanced.

- Accuse the targeted country of posing a threat to regional peace and stability.
- Impose economic sanctions to cripple and destabilize its economy. Do whatever possible to "make the economy scream." Give aid and money to subversive elements within the country.
- When the targeted government responds with angry criticisms about US aggression, treat such charges as evidence of hostility toward America.
- Deny harboring any aggressive designs; justify US actions as defensive measures against terrorism or communist aggrandizement or both.
- Attack the country with surrogate mercenary forces, trained, equipped, and financed by the US national security state or, if necessary, with regular US armed forces.

Not long after the Castro government took control of Cuba, Washington launched a campaign of CIA bombings and incendiary raids piloted by exiled Cubans stationed on American soil. Attorney General Robert Kennedy oversaw paramilitary operations, punitive economic measures, and sabotage aimed at undoing the new régime.[5]

As part of its campaign to overthrow Marxist rule in Havana, the United States launched an invasion of Cuba in April 1961. About 1,600 Cuban émigrés, trained and financed by the CIA, and assisted by hundreds of US military "advisors," established a beachhead at Bahia de los Cochinos (Bay of Pigs). In the words of one of their leaders, Manuel de Varona, their intent was to overthrow Castro and set up "a provisional government" to "restore all properties to the rightful owners."[6]

In the United States, with its reputedly free press, evidence of the coming invasion was suppressed by the Associated Press, United

Press International, and all the major newspapers and news weeklies, seventy-five of which—in an impressively unanimous act of self-censorship—rejected a report offered by the editors of the *Nation,* a liberal weekly, detailing US preparations for the attack upon Cuba.[7]

Fidel Castro's accusation that US rulers were planning to invade Cuba was dismissed by the *New York Times* as "shrill ... anti-American propaganda," and by *Time* magazine as Castro's "continued tawdry little melodrama of invasion."[8] When Washington broke diplomatic relations with Cuba in January 1961, the *New York Times* explained, "What snapped US patience was a new propaganda offense from Havana charging that the United States was plotting an 'imminent invasion' of Cuba."[9] Yet in fact, the invasion was imminent and did happen.

The invaders failed to penetrate beyond the Bay of Pigs and were driven off with heavy losses within several days. Over 1,110 prisoners were taken by the Cuban government. These men, all Cuban émigrés, were returned to the United States about six months later in exchange for a $60 million indemnity (referred to in the US press as a "ransom").

Such is the predominance of anticommunist orthodoxy that, after the Bay of Pigs invasion, there was no critical discussion in the United States regarding its moral and legal impropriety. Instead, commentary focused exclusively on tactical questions. There were repeated references to the disappointing "fiasco" and "disastrous attempt" to free Cuba from the "communist yoke." No mention that the invasion failed not because of insufficient air coverage, as some of the invaders claimed, but because the Cuban people, instead of rising en masse to join the counterrevolutionary expedition as anticipated by US leaders, closed ranks behind their revolution.

Among the Cuban-exile invaders taken prisoner near the Bay of Pigs (according to the Cuban government) were men whose families between them had previously owned 914,859 acres of land, 9,666 houses, 70 factories, 5 mines, 2 banks, and 10 sugar mills in Cuba.[10] They were the scions of the privileged class of prerevolutionary Cuba who had lived so comfortably under the Batista dictatorship, coming back to reclaim their substantial holdings. But in the US media they were hailed as nothing less than "freedom fighters."

Why would the Cuban people stand by the "Castro dictatorship"? That was never explained to the American public. Nothing much was said in the US press about the advances made by ordinary Cubans after the revolution, the millions who for the first time had a guaranteed right to a job, medical care, sufficient food, housing, education, and other public services—all of which were far from perfect but still composing a better life than the free market misery endured under the US-sponsored Batista ancien régime.

Nonfalsifiable Hostility

US rulers repeatedly condemned Cuba for being a tool of Soviet aggression. Now that the Soviet Union no longer exists, Cuba is still subjected to a US embargo. Because of the embargo, Cuba has the highest import-export tonnage costs of any country in the world, having to buy its school buses and medical supplies from far-off countries rather than from nearby United States, a would-be natural trading partner. Better relations with Washington would bring the Cubans more commerce, technology, and tourism, and a chance to reduce their burdensome defense expenditures. Yet Havana's overtures for friendlier relations have been repeatedly rebuffed by successive administrations in Washington. Refusing to be treated as a satellite of the US empire, Cuba is to be treated as an enemy.

If Washington justified its own hostility on the grounds that Cuba was hostile toward the United States, what became the justification when the Cuban government repeatedly tried to be friendly?

The US response has been to characterize the diplomatic overtures as deceptive ploys.

Years ago in the 1980s, when Havana requested normalized relations with the United States, the *New York Times* ran a "news analysis" headlined "What's Behind Castro's Softer Tone." The headline itself suggested that Castro was up to something. The opening sentence read, "Once again Fidel Castro is talking as if he wants to improve relations with the United States" ("as if," not actually). According to the *Times,* Castro was interested in "taking advantage" of US trade, technology, and tourism and would "prefer not to be spending so much time and energy on national defense." Here seemed to be a promising basis for improved relations. Fidel Castro was saying that Cuba's own self-interest rested on friendlier diplomatic and economic ties with Washington and not, as the United States claimed, on aggression and aggrandizement. Nevertheless, the *Times* analysis made nothing of Castro's stated desire to ease tensions and instead presented the rest of the story from the US government's perspective. It noted that most Washington officials "seem skeptical.... The Administration continues to believe that the best way to deal with the Cuban leader is with unyielding firmness.... Administration officials see little advantage in wavering."[11]

The article did not explain what justified Washington's "skeptical" stance, or why a blanket negative response to Castro should be described as "unyielding firmness" rather than, say, "hostile rigidity." Nor did it say why a willingness to make a positive response to his diplomatic overture must be labeled "wavering." It left readers with the impressions that the sneaky power-hungry Castro was out to get something from us but that our vigilant leaders were not about to be taken in. There was no explanation of what the United States had to lose if it entered closer relations with Cuba.

In short, the imperial stance is immune to evidence. If the Cubans angrily condemn Yankee aggression, this is proof of their hostility and diabolic design. If they act in a friendly manner and ask for negotiated settlements, showing a willingness to make concessions and cooperate in measures against terrorism, then it is assumed they are up to something and are resorting to trickery and manipulation. The US position is nonfalsifiable: both A and not-A serve as justification for the same hostile policy toward Cuba.

With the loss of Soviet aid and the continued US blockade, Cuba faced exceptionally hard times, what party leaders termed "the Special Period." Acknowledging the high unemployment and other hardships, Raul Castro, Fidel's younger brother, was quoted as saying that Cuba would move "toward a better form of socialism and ... a more democratic society."[12] (After Fidel Castro's protracted illness and retirement in 2008, Raul took over as president.) Raul's view of democracy did not include the multi-party, money-driven, electoral ballyhoo found in the United States. He seemed to envision a central role for the Communist Party but with greater room for debate and popular inputs.

Due to the US embargo and the cessation of Soviet aid, Cuba was unable to continue with a high-tech, high-fuel farming system. Searching for a way to feed its population, the island nation embarked upon an organic agricultural system that included oxen instead of tractors, organic planting instead of chemical fertilizers, organic pest control instead of pesticide spraying, and extensive use of urban gardens. Cuba developed a successful organic food system of interest to organic farmers from other countries. Here was the largest conversion from chemicalized agriculture to organic or semi-organic farming in human history.[13]

To US rulers, things like organic farming were of secondary consideration, if that. What Washington continued to demand was that Cuban leaders "liberalized" their economy, that is, *privatized* it, replacing the public sector with a corporate-dominated profit-driven sector that would be integrated into the global investment system. Then and only then would Cuba no longer be demonized.

One-Way Freedom

US policymakers have long condemned Cuba for its controlled press. Cubans, we are told, do not enjoy the open discourse said to be found in the "free and independent" US media. In fact, if it counts for anything, the average Cuban has more access to Western news sources than the average American has to Cuban sources. Cuba is bombarded with US broadcasting, including Voice of America, regular Spanish-language stations direct from Miami, and a US-government propaganda station called Radio Marti. Havana has asked that Cuba be allowed a frequency for Cuban use in the United States, something Washington has refused to do. In response to those who attack the lack of dissent in the Cuban media, Fidel Castro promised to open up the Cuban press to all opponents of the revolution on the day he saw US communists enjoying regular exposure in the US major media—an offer the freedom-loving Washington policymakers refused to consider.

Cuba has also been condemned for not allowing its people to flee the island. That so many want to depart is treated as proof that Cuban socialism is a harshly repressive system, rather than that the US embargo has made life markedly difficult in Cuba. No mention is made of the lures that for forty years have been offered to Cuban émigrés who make it to the United States: public-assistance cash payments, Medicare, scholarships, and low-interest college and business loans.

Millions of people want to flee *capitalist* countries like Mexico, Colombia, Pakistan, India, Nigeria, Poland, El Salvador, Haiti, Philippines, Indonesia, Macedonia, and others too numerous to list, but this is never treated as grounds for questioning the free market system that inflicts such misery upon them. Imagine if the United States were thrown open to all Mexicans who wanted to come, with a guarantee of generous government monetary support. The human tide would be awesome, especially as the free-trade poverty inflicted upon that nation only worsens living conditions. As it is, illegal immigration from capitalist Mexico already has become a major issue in the United States.

In the early 1980s, in accordance with an agreement between Havana and Washington, the Cuban government allowed its citizens to depart for the United States if they had US visas. Washington agreed to issue 20,000 visas a year but in fact granted only a few, failing to live up to the agreement. But Cubans who fled illegally on skimpy crafts or hijacked vessels and planes produced better propaganda value. Hailed as heroes who had risked their lives to escape communist tyranny, they were readily granted asylum.

Given the hardships of the Special Period, most of the émigrés departed Cuba for economic rather than political reasons. A leaked memorandum from the US Interests Section in Havana to the US Secretary of State admitted that a substantial majority of Cuban refugees applied for entry visas "more because of the deteriorating economic situation than a real fear of persecution." The memorandum noted that applications submitted by Cuban human rights groups "lack demonstrable evidence of persecution.... Almost none show proof of house searches, interrogations, detention, or arrest."[14]

When Havana announced it would let anyone leave who wanted to, the Clinton administration reverted to a closed-door policy, fearing an immigration tide. Policymakers voiced concern that the "escape" of too many disgruntled refugees would help Castro stay in power by easing tensions within Cuban society. In brief, Cuba was condemned both for not allowing its citizens to leave and then for allowing them to go.

US policymakers regularly fail to live up to the high moral principles to which they pay lip service. Thus while claiming to be fighting terrorism, they gave sanctuary and shelter to the likes of Luis Posada Carriles and Orlando Bosch, admitted assassins and perpetrators of the plot that blew up a Cuban civilian airliner in 1976, killing all 76 people aboard. The 1971 Montreal Convention mandates that persons charged with destroying a civilian aircraft in flight are to be extradited to face trial. The US government signed the Montreal Convention but still refused to hand over Carriles and Bosch, both of whom ended up living comfortably in the United States.[15]

In contrast, Havana sent five agents to the United States to observe and report on the violent plots aimed at Cuba by exile groups in Florida, including the bombings of tourist hotels in Cuba to disrupt its economy—terrorist acts perpetrated against civilian targets with the full knowledge of the US national security state. The five undertook this mission after Washington ignored Havana's appeals to stop the attacks.[16] The Cuban agents were eventually caught and have been imprisoned in the United States for over twelve years, in some cases facing life imprisonment with no hope of release. None of the Cuban Five ever committed an act of espionage, sabotage, or terrorism. All they did was provide intelligence to their government so that it might defend itself against impending CIA-supported terrorist attacks.[17]

Consistent Inconsistencies

While attending a World Affairs Council meeting in San Francisco a few years ago, I heard some participants refer to the irony of Cuba's having come "full circle" since the days before the revolution. In prerevolutionary Havana, the best hotels and shops were reserved for the foreign tourists and the relatively few Cubans who had Yankee dollars. Today it is the same, these "foreign policy experts" gleefully observed.

This judgment overlooks some important differences. Strapped for hard currency, the revolutionary government elected to take advantage of its beautiful beaches and sunny climate to develop a tourist industry. Today, tourism is one of Cuba's most important sources of hard currency, if not the most important.

True, tourists are given hotel accommodations that most Cubans cannot afford. But in prerevolutionary Cuba, the profits from tourism were pocketed by big corporations, generals, gamblers, and mobsters. Today the profits are split between the foreign investors who build and manage the hotels and the Cuban government. The portion going to the government helps to pay for health clinics, education, the importation of fuel, and the like. In other words, through the public sector, the people reap much of the benefits of the tourist trade—as is true of the export earnings from Cuba's sugar, coffee, tobacco, rum, seafood, honey, nickel, and marble industries.

If Cuba were in exactly the same place as before the revolution, completely under satellite-state servitude, Washington would have lifted the embargo and embraced Havana. When the Cuban government no longer redistributes a major portion of the surplus value to the common populace, when it allows all surplus wealth to be pocketed by a few rich corporate owners, and when it returns the factories and lands to a small opulent owning class—as the former communist countries of Eastern Europe have done—then it will have come full circle, returning to a privatized, free market servitude. And then will it be warmly embraced by Washington as have the Eastern European nations.

Western policymakers say as much. In 1994 I wrote a letter to then-Representative Lee Hamilton, chair of the House Foreign Affairs Committee, urging a normalization of relations with Cuba. He wrote back that US policy toward Cuba should be "updated" in order to be "more effective," and that "we must put Cuba in contact with the ideas and practice of democracy ... and *the economic benefits of a free market system* [italics added]." The US blockade, Hamilton went on, was put in place to "promote democratic change in Cuba and retaliate for the large-scale seizure of American assets by the Castro régime."

Needless to say, Hamilton did not explain why his own government—which had supported the prerevolutionary Batista dictatorship in Cuba for decades—was now suddenly so insistent on installing western-style democracy in that country. The revealing thing in his letter was his explicit acknowledgment that Washington's policy was dedicated to advancing the cause of the "free market system" and retaliating for the "large-scale seizure of American assets." In so many words, he was letting us know that a core commitment of US policy was to make the world safe for corporate investments and profits.

Those who do not believe that our rulers are consciously dedicated to the propagation of transnational corporate capitalism (even after they say they are) should note how they explicitly press for "free market reforms" in one country after another. We no longer have to impute such intentions to them. Almost all their actions, and with increasing frequency their own words, testify to what they have been doing.

When forced to choose between democracy without capitalism or capitalism without democracy, the empire builders unhesitatingly embrace the latter, although they also prefer the legitimating cloak of a limited and money-driven "democracy" when possible. Such is the face of imperialism.

9

Satellites or Enemies

THE FACE OF IMPERIALISM TODAY is of an American empire reaching into every corner of the world, served by cooperative "allies" and other satellite nations, an empire whose transnational corporations control the markets, investments, and resources of entire regions, accumulating hundreds of billions of dollars in yearly profits.

One would think that such a colossus could rest on its achievements, having enjoyed such smashing success in wiping out almost all revolutionary and reformist movements while securing the global supremacy of its corporate moneyed class. Instead we hear that dangers still abound, aimed at the United States or the "western world" in general. For decades the mortal threat was the communists; today it is the nationalist extremists, Islamic jihadists, and mad dictators of various lineage. Enemies are forever conjured to stir fear in the hearts of the American people so that they might continue to support a US imperium that bleeds the republic in order to rule the planet.

Yugoslavia: Privatization by Bombing

Far from being wedded to each other as claimed, capitalism and democracy are often on a collision course. US rulers find electoral democracy useful when it helps to destabilize one-party socialism or derail a reformist movement or when it serves as a legitimating cloak for capitalist restoration. But when democracy starts to successfully advance egalitarian economic reforms, when it becomes a *barrier* to an untrammeled capitalism, then it must be undone or diluted in some way.

A striking example is Yugoslavia. Multi-ethnic Yugoslavia was once a regional industrial success, with a fairly high economic growth rate, free medical care, a literacy rate over 90 percent, and a relatively equitable and prosperous economic life for its various peoples. Despite a considerable amount of private foreign investment, the Yugoslav economy was still mostly publicly owned, with a large public sector that was out of line with the march toward free market Third Worldization.

That US leaders planned to dismember Yugoslavia is not a matter of speculation but of public record. As early as 1984, the Reagan administration issued US National Security Decision Directive 133: United States Policy Towards Yugoslavia, stamped "secret sensitive." It followed an earlier directive that called for a "quiet revolution" to overthrow communist governments while "reintegrating the countries of Eastern Europe into the orbit of the World market" (that is, the capitalist world market). The economic "reforms" pressed upon Yugoslavia by the IMF and other foreign creditors mandated that all socially owned firms and all worker-managed production units be transformed into private corporate enterprises.[1] To best accomplish this goal, Yugoslavia itself had to be dismembered.

There came years of US-led boycott, embargo, and wars of secession with US-financed secessionist forces leading various republics to break away from Yugoslavia. In February 1999, western officials made their dedication to privatization perfectly clear, issuing an ultimatum stating: "The economy of Kosovo [a major province of Serbia] shall function in accordance with free market principles." All matters of trade and corporate ownership were to be left to the private market.[2]

Then in March–June 1999 came eleven weeks of round-the-clock US aerial attacks against Serbia, Kosovo, and Montenegro, leaving the Yugoslav economy in ruins. The private corporate sites within Yugoslavia were left untouched by the attackers. The bombs fell only on state-owned or worker-controlled factories, enterprises, auto plants, construction firms, municipal power stations and other public utilities, government radio and television stations, depots, ports, railroads, bridges, water supply systems, hotels, housing projects, hospitals, schools, and hundreds of other nonmilitary state-owned targets—in what amounted to *privatization by bombing*. What?. C'mon....

In addition, there were some 8,500 civilian casualties, and hundreds of thousands of tons of highly toxic chemicals spewed into the air, soil, and water, including depleted uranium in the Danube River, a source of drinking water for millions of people.[3] The US bombing of Yugoslavia was a war crime that went unpunished and almost unnoticed. As George Kenney, a former State Department official under the elder Bush administration, commented, "Dropping cluster bombs on highly populated urban areas doesn't result in accidental fatalities. It is purposeful terror bombing."[4]

The American public was smothered with stories, many of them fabricated, demonizing the Serbian people and their elected leaders as the perpetrators of mass rape and "genocide."[5] More likely, the Serbs were targeted because they were the largest ethnic group in the federation and the most committed to keeping the country together, with a working class that was most firmly socialist. Yugoslavia's democratically elected president, Slobodan Milošević, who presided over a coalition government, was portrayed as a bloodthirsty tyrant and

"Serbian nationalist." In fact, Milošević and his wife, Mira Marković, herself an active player in Yugoslav national politics, had long argued *for* multi-ethnic unity and *against* nationalistic supremacy of any stripe (including Serbian nationalism).[6]

All sides in the secessionist wars committed atrocities, but incidents of Croat and Muslim war crimes against the Serbs rarely made it into the US press, and when they did they were accorded minimal mention.[7] John Ranz, chair of Survivors of the Buchenwald Concentration Camp, USA, asked where were the TV cameras when hundreds of Serbs were slaughtered by Muslims near Srebrenica?[8]

The Serbs were charged with "ethnic cleansing." But any number of Western sources including the EU, various UN commissions, Western security agencies, the German Foreign Ministry, UN generals, former State Department officials, Spanish and FBI forensic teams were unable to find evidence of genocide. Nor did the international tribunal set up by the NATO powers succeed in showing Milošević guilty of such a charge.[9]

In 2000, at the initiative of the European Union, a Stability Pact for Southeastern Europe was set up to create (in its own words) "vibrant market economies" in the Balkans. The Overseas Private Investment Corporation inaugurated a fund "to provide capital for new business development, expansion and privatization."[10] Meanwhile, the US Agency for International Development announced the undertaking of "assistance programs to ... advance Montenegro toward a free market economy."[11]

In April 2001, according to the London *Financial Times,* the newly installed "pro-West" rulers of Yugoslavia (by now reduced to Serbia and Montenegro), beneficiaries of millions of dollars in US electoral funds, launched "a comprehensive privatization program as part of economic reforms introduced following the overthrow of former president Slobodan Milošević." This included the sale of more than 7,000 publicly owned companies to private investors.[12]

The once viable and fairly prosperous social democracy of Yugo-slavia was now broken into a cluster of right-wing mini-republics in which everything was privatized and deregulated. Living standards dropped drastically; the public infrastructure was reduced to shambles; unemployment and poverty skyrocketed; and a new class of rich in-vestors strutted upon the political stage, including shady coteries of Kosovar Albanians who, as reported by Interpol, held "the largest share of the heroin market" in Switzerland, Austria, Belgium, Germany, Hungary, and several other countries.[13]

All sorts of US liberals and other "leftists," who later opposed the war against a dictator and torturer like Saddam Hussein in Iraq, *supported* the war against a social democracy like Yugoslavia. They stood shoulder to shoulder with the White House, NATO, the CIA, the Pentagon, the IMF, and the mainstream media, convinced that they were opposing the demonic Serbs in a "humanitarian" war—a war that brought the restoration of free market corporate capitalism.[14]

Iraq: Régime Change the Hard Way

In the face of massive demonstrations around the world against an impending US invasion of Iraq, President George W. Bush and other members of his administration gave varied reasons to justify their aggression in March 2003. They claimed that Saddam Hussein was developing weapons of mass destruction and had close ties with the Al Qaeda terrorist organization. Both charges were rejected by congres-sional committees and UN inspection teams as unfounded.[15]

Another pretext for invasion: Saddam had committed war crimes, including the attack against Iran and the gassing of Kurds at Halabja. But the Pentagon's own study found that the massacre of Kurds was committed by the Iranians, not the Iraqis.[16] And in the war against Iran, occurring over twenty years earlier in 1980, Iraq received tactical assistance, helicopter gunships, and chemical and biological weapons from the United States.[17]

Having seen that the reasons given by the White House to justify an invasion of Iraq were highly questionable, some observers incorrectly concluded that the administration was simply befuddled. Because the Bush policymakers misled the public, it was assumed that they themselves were misled. Never considered was the likelihood that Bush et al. were *lying* in order to cloak the agenda of their own imperial class. The Iraq War has been of good service for a number of powerful interests.

A little history is in order. In 1958 a revolution in Iraq, led by a broad democratic coalition, kicked out the British and American oil companies and initiated popular reforms and democratic rule. Ten years later, the Ba'ath party seized power, with Saddam Hussein serving as point man for the CIA, torturing and murdering every democrat, reformer, constitutionalist, and communist the Ba'athists could get hold of, including the left wing of their own party. During the years Saddam committed his worst atrocities, he was Washington's poster boy. All this the US press let slip down the memory hole, never to be retrieved. Ever since the Gulf War of 1991, Saddam has been portrayed as a maniacal dictator as bad as Hitler.[18] Why so? *Are you kidding me?*

The last thing that US rulers want in the Middle East is independent, self-developing nations that control their own economies and natural resources. The Iraq economy under Saddam was entirely state-owned, a "Stalinist economy," cried US Secretary of Defense Donald Rumsfeld. Upon coming to power, Saddam Hussein committed the sin of *economic nationalism.* Instead of acting as a vassal, he pursued policies of national development, even retaining some of the social programs of the earlier democratic government. In fact, "per capita income doubled in the 1970s, and the government spent heavily to improve education and health services."[19] As of 1990, Iraq had the highest standard of living in the Middle East.

The empire tries to prevent the emergence of any competing superpower or even any potentially competing *regional* power charting a course of its own.[20] If Iraq would not be a compliant client state, a satellite, then it would have to be targeted as a potential enemy. The country was subjected to years of US-led sanctions and aerial attacks (1990–2003) that wreaked havoc on its economy and people. Months before the March 2003 invasion, the White House put together a committee whose sole purpose was to supervise the impending privatization and deregulation of the Iraqi economy.

After the US invasion, most of that economy was destroyed, shut down, or privatized at giveaway prices. Looters were let loose on Iraq's government ministries and headquarters; all state-owned factories, hotels, supermarkets, and many hospitals; and most public universities, including engineering and nursing colleges.[21] The Iraq Federation of Trade Unions was raided and destroyed by the US military, its leaders and members arrested and imprisoned.[22]

The invaders also resorted to the systematic destruction of Iraqi culture, by encouraging museums to be looted of their priceless treasures, while libraries were burned, and academics were murdered.[23] Poverty and underemployment climbed precipitously, so too the Iraqi national debt as international loans were floated in order to help the Iraqis pay for their own misery. At the same time, depleted uranium weaponry caused a drastic rise in cancer rates in Iraq (as in Afghanistan). The US invasion brought Iraq firmly back into the free market sphere as a destitute satellite state.[24]

Saddam Hussein had posed other problems. In November 2000 he stopped accepting US dollars as payment for Iraq's oil exports and started accepting the euro as a reserve currency. Up to then, the dollar had retained its value because it was the international standard in oil transactions. Were more countries to divest themselves of their dollar reserves, the massive glut of dollars on the world market would cause still more countries to switch to euros. US deficits would become unserviceable; the dollar would collapse in value; and the US economy would end in shambles. By conquering Iraq and installing a vassal state, Washington could guarantee that Iraqi oil exports were again dollar valued.[25]

Another reason for targeting Iraq can be summed up in one word: *oil.* As of late 2002 Saddam had offered exploratory concessions to several countries other than the United States. The postinvasion puppet régime installed by Washington reneged on those agreements, of course. With a reserve of 113 billion barrels of quality crude, Iraq's supply comes to many trillions of dollars, potentially the biggest resource grab in history. Vice President Dick Cheney remarked that the nation controlling Middle East oil can exercise a "stranglehold" over the world economy.[26]

Earlier, during the 1990s, because of the slumping price of crude, US leaders were interested in keeping Iraqi oil off the market. The *San Francisco Chronicle* headlined a story: "Iraq's Oil Poses Threat to the West." If Iraq reentered the international oil market, the *Chronicle* reported, "it would devalue British North Sea oil, undermine American oil production and—much more important—it would destroy the huge profits which the United States [read: US oil companies] stands to gain from its massive investment in Caucasian oil production."[27] Direct control of Iraqi oil was the surest way to keep it off the world market when the price was not right, and the surest way to profit from its eventual sale when the price picked up.

The prolonged occupation of Iraq also created a whole new bonanza for US corporate contractors. Billions of dollars in war contracts brought in astronomical profits for hundreds of private companies, augmented even more by brazen corruption. As much as one-third to one-half of the immense funds allocated by Congress for the Iraqi war remained unaccounted for.[28]

Still another reason for régime change in Iraq was concern for Israel. The neoconservative officials in the Bush Jr. administration—Paul Wolfowitz, Douglas Feith, Elliot Abrams, Robert Kagan, and others—were strong proponents of an expansionist strain of Zionism linked closely to the right-wing Likud Party of Israel. Assisted by the powerfully financed Israeli lobby, they pushed for war with Iraq well before the September 11, 2001, attack on the World Trade Center.[29] Saddam Hussein was Israel's most consistent adversary in the Middle East, providing political and financial support to the Palestinian resistance.

In sum, the invasion and destruction of Iraq was not a foolish mistake. It certainly was not a quick and easy victory as expected, but overall it served the plutocracy quite well, at a horrific price to the people of Iraq (and a heavy price for the US taxpayer). William Blum sums it up:

The people of that unhappy land have lost everything—their homes, their schools, their electricity, their clean water, their environment, their neighborhoods, their mosques, their archaeology, their jobs, their careers, their professionals, their state-run enterprises, their physical health, their mental health, their health care, their welfare state, their women's rights, their religious tolerance, their safety, their security, their children, their parents, their past, their present, their future, their lives. More than half the population [is] either dead, wounded, traumatized, in prison, internally displaced, or in foreign exile. The air, soil, water, blood and genes drenched with depleted uranium [are bringing] the most awful birth defects.... A river of blood runs alongside the Euphrates and Tigris, through a country that may never be put back together again.[30]

North Korea: "Sanity" at the Brink

Like others who have had the temerity to chart an independent course, the rulers of the Democratic People's Republic of Korea (DPRK, or North Korea) have been routinely described by our policymakers and pundits as mentally imbalanced. Senior Defense Department officials refer to the DPRK as a country "not of this planet," led by "dysfunctional" autocrats. One US government official suggested that they might be "really totally crazy."[31]

In addition, North Korea has been characterized as a most sinister power. To be sure, there have been things about the DPRK that can give one pause, including its dynastic leadership system, its highly dictatorial one-party rule, and the chaos that seems implanted in its "planned" economy. By 2010, North Korea was undergoing a sharp currency devaluation that was wiping out people's savings and making life still harder.[32]

Less publicized in the US media were North Korea's repeated overtures, dating from the early 1990s, for a bilateral nonaggression pact with the United States, all rejected by Washington. In 2006 the DPRK grandly announced that it had successfully conducted a nuclear weapons test; another test followed in 2009. Were the North Koreans playing brinkmanship, or did they know something about US global policy that US rulers preferred to leave unsaid? In short, *the United States has never attacked or invaded any nation that has a nuclear arsenal* (except for the NATO bombing forays into Pakistan during the Afghanistan conflict).

Of the numerous countries directly battered by US-supported military actions in the decades after World War II, none wielded a nuclear deterrence at the time they were attacked. During the Korean War (1950–1953), the United States carpet-bombed the North without stint and with impunity, dropping more explosives (635,000 tons and 32,557 tons of napalm) than in the entire Pacific theater during World War II, without the slightest concern for the immense toll taken on civilian life and the North's infrastructure.[33]

Consider more recent events. In the aftermath of 9/11, US president George W. Bush claimed the right to initiate any military action against any "terrorist" nation, organization, or individual of his choosing, thereby transforming the president into something of an absolute monarch who could exercise life-and-death power over any quarter of the Earth, regardless of international law and the US Constitution.[34] Needless to say, numerous nations—the DPRK among them—were discomforted by the president's self-elevation to King of the Planet. *WOW.*

It was only in 2008 that President Bush finally removed North Korea from a list of states that allegedly sponsor terrorism. But from Pyongyang's viewpoint, there remained another more devilishly disquieting hit list. In December 2001, two months after 9/11, Vice President Dick Cheney referred chillingly to "forty or fifty countries" that might need "military disciplining."[35] A month later in his 2002 State of the Union message, President Bush pruned the list down to Iraq, Iran, and North Korea, three culprits who, he said, composed an *axis of evil*.

First to get hit was Iraq, nation #1 of the axis of evil in a war that has reduced that country to shambles. North Korea could not help but notice what was happening to Iraq, nor could it overlook the subsequent threats directed at Iran, axis nation #2. Rather than passively await its fate sitting in Washington's crosshairs as nation #3 on the US hit list, the DPRK began boldly announcing that it had a "powerful nuclear deterrence" ready to use if necessary.[36] Such bluster—obviously designed to act as a defense—was characterized in US official circles and media as wild aggression. In May 2009, Secretary of State Hillary Clinton warned that the United States would not be "blackmailed by North Korea." Defense Secretary Robert Gates fulminated, "We will not stand idly by as North Korea builds the capability to wreak destruction on any target in Asia—or on us." President Obama condemned the DPRK's "unacceptable" and "belligerent behavior" as posing a "grave threat." [37]

In June 2009, the UN Security Council unanimously passed a US-sponsored resolution ratcheting up the financial, trade, and military sanctions against North Korea, a nation already hard hit by sanctions. In response to this action, Kim Jong-il's government announced it would no longer "even think about giving up its nuclear weapons" and would produce still more of them.

US leaders refused to guarantee that they would not try to topple Pyongyang's communist government. There was talk of putting the DPRK back on the list of state sponsors of terrorism, though Secretary Clinton admitted that there was no evidence to support such a designation.[38]

From its lonely and precarious perch North Korea could not help feeling somewhat vulnerable. The DPRK's outdated and ill-equipped army was no match for the conventional forces of the United States, South Korea, and Japan. The United States maintained a large attack base in South Korea. At least once a year the US military conducted joint exercises with South Korean forces, practicing a land invasion of the North. The US Air Force had nuclear arsenals in Okinawa, Guam, and Hawaii. Japan not only said it could produce nuclear bombs within a year, it seemed increasingly willing to do so.[39]

The DPRK's nuclear arsenal is a two-edged sword. It might deter attack or invite attack. It might cause US officials to think twice before cinching a tighter knot around the North, or it might cause Washington to move aggressively toward a risky confrontation. After years of encirclement and demonization by Washington, the Pyongyang leaders were convinced that the best way to deter superpower aggression was by developing a nuclear arsenal. It does not really sound so crazy. Having been pushed to the brink for so long, the North Koreans by 2010 were taking a gamble, pursuing an arguably "sane" deterrence policy in the otherwise insane world configured by a voracious empire.

Iran: Evil Threat du Jour

Were it not that Iraq proved to be such an endless and costly venture, the United States would have moved long ago against Iran, #2 on the axis-of-evil hit list. As early as January 2005 Vice President Cheney was accusing Iran of sponsoring terrorism against Americans and building a "fairly robust new nuclear program" that threatened Middle East stability and world peace. Iran might emerge as a dominant power in the region and—as with Iraq—we must not allow that to happen, Cheney warned.[40] In 2007, according to one Washington official, the vice president was holding meetings in his office on "how to create a casus belli between Tehran and Washington."[41]

Iran had other traits akin to pre-invasion Iraq: a high literacy rate, a better than usual Third-World living standard, a recycling of some of the oil profits into the social wage, and a leadership that was charting an independent course. And as we might expect, Iranian president Mahmoud Ahmadinejad was diagnosed by US media pundits as "dangerously unstable" and "crazy"(except for those commentators who saw him as devilishly "cunning"). *Um . . . he IS crazy!*

All sorts of caveats were directed at Tehran for having pursued an enriched uranium program—which every nation in the world has a right to do. It was repeatedly assumed by US and Israeli leaders that Iran would want a nuclear program for the purpose of building bombs. In fact, Tehran planned to make the country less oil-dependent by building nuclear power plants. Iran was the world's fifth largest exporter of crude oil, but its crude reserves were likely to run out within twenty years. Even today, the lack of refining capacity forces the Iranians to import about 30 percent of their gasoline.[42]

By 2007 the US Navy was stopping Iranian ships to check for arms shipments. US secret operatives were training Iranian mercenaries to spy, recruit, and conduct terrorist attacks within that country. Washington also imposed economic and political sanctions on Tehran.[43] The Pentagon announced that 10,000 sites in Iran had been mapped and targeted for aerial destruction, a threat reiterated by the Obama White House in 2010. President Obama augmented the already massive military buildup with nuclear-armed Trident submarines and two

US carrier groups capable of delivering death and destruction upon Iran and its eighty million inhabitants.[44]

These increasingly menacing threats were in violation of UN Security Council Resolution 1887 (September 2009), which requires nation-states to peacefully resolve disputes related to nuclear issues, in accordance with the ban laid down by the UN Charter on the use or threat of force.[45] Meanwhile, in a moment of truth, the CIA stated its inability to find credible evidence that Iran posed any kind of threat to the United States, nuclear or otherwise.[46]

In 2009 Obama stated, "No single nation should pick and choose which nation holds nuclear weapons."[47] But that is exactly what the United States was trying to do in regard to a benighted North Korea and Iran. The US policy has been to maintain and expand its own immense nuclear arsenal while pressuring other nations to refrain from developing such weapons. The empire never has to abide by rules it imposes on others.[48]

Venezuela: The Threat of Socialistic Reforms

Not long after being elected president of Venezuela in 1998, Hugo Chávez was being denounced as a dictator and a threat to "American interests" by US rulers and their faithful mouthpieces in the mainstream media. Chávez had the audacity to initiate major political-economic reforms on behalf of the Venezuelan working populace. Successive earlier administrations, dominated by the super rich, had done nothing about the rampant corruption, the growing gap between rich and poor, and the worsening malnutrition and desperation among the lowest stratum. The neoliberal market "adjustments" of the 1980s and 1990s only made things worse, cutting social spending and eliminating subsidies in consumer goods. In response to those horrendous conditions, here are some of the measures taken by the Chávez government:

- A land reform program was installed to assist small farmers and the landless poor. A large estate owned by a British beef company was occupied by agrarian workers for farming purposes. Corn and other crops have been cultivated to make Venezuela more self-sufficient in food.
- The government set up a marine conservation program and began taking steps to protect the land and fishing rights of indigenous peoples. Earlier administrations allowed transnational corporations to massively contaminate Venezuela's lakes and rivers, while stripping its forests. The Chávez government launched reforestation and restoration programs, with sustainable use of forest lands. Over 5,000 Conservation Committees with over 3,000 greenhouses have raised tens of millions of tree seedlings on vast stretches of previously depleted lands.
- Many children from poor families never attended school for they could not afford the annual fees. Education is now completely free (up to the university level), causing a dramatic increase in enrollment. For the very poorest children, school lunch is their best meal of the day.
- Special state-financed banks now assist small enterprises, farmers, and a growing number of worker cooperatives (many run by women). New "socialist supermarkets" provide quality foods at discount prices in poor neighborhoods.
- Neighborhood committees known as "Bolivarian Circles" have been organized throughout the nation to activate citizens at the community level to assist in literacy and health campaigns and public repair jobs.
- Under Chávez, a health program greatly assisted by Cuban doctors and dentists has reached millions of people who never could afford medical treatment. Chávez also put Venezuelan military doctors and dentists to work in the free clinics. Much of the Venezuelan medical establishment vehemently opposed

the program, seeing it as a Cuban communist campaign to undermine physicians' private earnings.

- The government halted further attempts at privatizing the state-run oil industry—80 percent of which was still publicly owned.
- Chávez kicked out the U.S. military advisors and prohibited overflights by U.S. military aircraft engaged in counterinsurgency in Colombia.
- A new communal police force is making strides in reducing crime in Caracas. Several years after the US Drug Enforcement Administration was expelled from the country (for interfering with internal affairs unrelated to drug enforcement), Venezuelan authorities have apprehended forty-nine major narcotraffickers.
- In 2009, the Venezuelan Attorney General successfully prosecuted 2,700 cases of corruption. In addition, more than 17,000 cases relating to drug trafficking were prosecuted. Corruption has been a historic problem in the oil-rich country.[49]

Over the years, US agencies such as the National Endowment for Democracy and the Agency for International Development channeled millions of dollars to Venezuelan organizations that were highly critical of the Chávez government, including more than $4 million to journalists and corporate media in Venezuela as part of the campaign to promote régime change.[50] All this interference comes from an American government that itself does not allow foreign interests to spend one dollar in US elections.

In the US and Venezuelan media, Hugo Chávez was accorded the usual ad hominem treatment. The *San Francisco Chronicle* quoted a political opponent who called him "a psychopath, a terribly aggressive guy." The London *Financial Times* saw him as "increasingly autocratic" and presiding over a "rogue democracy." In the *Nation*, Marc

Cooper—one of those Cold War liberals who regularly defends the US empire—described Chávez as "a thug" who "flirts with megalomania" and whose behavior "borders on the paranoiac."[51]

Other media mouthpieces labeled Chávez "mercurial," "heavy-handed," "incompetent," "dictatorial," a "barracks populist," and, above all, a "leftist," a term that is seldom defined. In contrast, Chávez's opponents, free market plutocrats and military leaders of the privileged social order, who staged a treasonous coup in April 2002 against Venezuela's democratically elected government, are depicted in the United States as champions of "pro-democratic" and "pro-West" governance.[52] When one of these perpetrators, General Carlos Alfonzo, was hit with charges for the role he played in the undemocratic coup, the *New York Times* chose to call him a "dissident" whose rights were being suppressed by the Chávez government.[53]

Venezuela's wealthy media moguls, all vehemently anti-Chávez, own all the television stations save one and all the major newspapers. No wonder many Venezuelans know relatively little about government reforms. Andre Vltchek met numerous Venezuelan journalists in Caracas and in the provinces "who complained that they were not allowed to write articles and produce news programs that were supportive of their own government. Corporate media bosses threatened to fire those who would sympathize with Chávez."[54]

In 2007 Chávez refused to renew the license of Venezuela's oldest private station, RCTV, because of the active support it had given to the April 2002 coup against him. US opinion makers denounced him as a dictator.

Two letters by American readers commented on US media treatment of the Venezuelan president. In 2002 Donald Scott asked why the *San Francisco Chronicle* described Chávez in such loaded terms as "a populist strongman with leftist leanings." To be consistent, Scott argued, President Bush should be described as "an elitist oilman with far-right leanings who became president by political manipulation."

Scott concluded, "I doubt that we will ever see such candor by US newspapers."[55] Another reader, Robert Naiman, questioned the *New York Times*:

> I was puzzled by your article in which Venezuela's efforts to aid poor people in the Western Hemisphere, including Mexicans needing eye surgery and Americans needing heating oil, were described as "pet projects" of President Hugo Chávez. Don't all countries seek foreign allies? Why is it particularly nefarious for Venezuela to do so? Similar efforts by the United States government are described in the article as "development programs." Why are these not also "pet projects"? Why the asymmetry in your reporting?[56]

Millions of his compatriots correctly perceive Chávez as being the only president who has ever paid attention to the nation's poorest areas. His government represents an entirely different mode of social organization in which the nations of the world should put people before profits, using the wealth of the nation to serve the working populace instead of the favored few. For this, he and any other leader with such an egalitarian agenda are immediately listed in the "enemy" column by the ever-vigilant empire builders.

10

Rogue Imperium

"WILL THE FUTURE EVER ARRIVE?" Victor Hugo once asked. Maybe it has already passed us by. Perhaps the empire has moved too successfully to a point of no return, allowing little possibility of democratic transformation. Or maybe the boundless greed of the imperial plutocracy will become so oppressively and obviously burdensome as to cause the populace at home and abroad to chart a more humane and sustainable course.

A Successful Empire

Let us recapitulate some of the key points previously presented. US rulers are committed to maintaining "overwhelming unilateral global military dominance."[1] While claiming to be motivated by a dedication to human rights and democracy, US rulers have armed, trained, and financed some of the most notorious right-wing autocracies in history.

The overall aim is to promote a global order dedicated to private ownership of the world's financial and industrial wealth, expropriation of its natural resources, and advantageous control of its consumer and labor markets. This is a world where the gap between the wealthy few and the many poor grows ever greater, where the masses are experiencing a drastic decline in living standards.[2] The goal is a world composed *totally* of exploitative, repressive, free market countries like Indonesia, Nigeria, and Haiti rather than prosperous social democracies like Finland, Sweden, or Denmark (whatever their respective flaws). Thus far the empire builders have been quite successful.

Even the relatively prosperous social democracies of Western Europe and Scandinavia, with their generous benefits and high wages, may find it increasingly difficult to compete in an international market ruled by laissez-faire free trade agreements and crowded with an additional 1.47 billion workers injected into the global low-wage labor market over the past two decades from China, India, Southeast Asia, Eastern Europe, and the former Soviet Union.[3]

Some of the liberal cognoscenti are never happier than when they can patronizingly dilate on the malapropisms and "stupidity" of Ronald Reagan, George W. Bush, or other unlettered imperial policymakers. What I have tried to show is that US rulers have been neither retarded nor misdirected nor inept. To be sure, the 2003 invasion of Iraq sank into a quagmire not long after Bush announced "mission accomplished." At the operational level his administration made gross miscalculations. This means the imperialists are fallible but not mindless, strong but not omnipotent.

As we have seen, nations that chart a self-defining course, seeking to use their land, labor, natural resources, and markets as they see fit, free from the smothering embrace of the free market global order, are designated as enemies of the United States or a threat to "US national interests." Their leaders often have their moral sanity called into question, as has been the case at one time or another with Fidel Castro of Cuba, Manuel Noriega of Panama, Daniel Ortega of Nicaragua, Muammar al-Qaddafi of Libya, Jean-Bertrand Aristide of Haiti, Slobodan Milošević of Yugoslavia, Saddam Hussein of Iraq, Mahmoud Ahmadinejad of Iran, Hugo Chávez of Venezuela, and others.

When US policymakers keep providing new and different explanations to justify a particular action, they most likely are lying. When people keep changing their story, you can be fairly sure it's a story. This means that they are being not stupid but deceptive. So it is with most imperial policies.

As I have argued in this book, US global policy has been ruthlessly rational. Rather than deploring its failures, we should be deploring its successes because these "successes" do not represent the interests of the American people or the people of the world. We should spend less time talking about how "stupid" and "short-sighted" US foreign policy has been and more time exposing how successfully driven it is on behalf of the international plutocracy. Only then might we be able to change course.

Above International Law

The imperium is ruled not by fools but by liars, manipulators, murderers, and other criminals—all of whom tend to believe in their own virtue. The imperial state often functions accountable to no one. Wars of aggression are a crime against international law and a crime against humanity. And such crimes were committed when US leaders launched invasions against Vietnam, Laos, Cambodia, Somalia, Grenada, Panama, Iraq, Afghanistan, and various other countries; and when they sponsored wars of attrition against civilian targets in Mozambique, Angola, Nicaragua, El Salvador, Guatemala, Yugoslavia, and scores of other places, leaving hundreds of thousands dead. The US empire asserts the right to invade and devastate any country for preemptive reasons, under the *National Security Strategy* (September 2002).[4] No communist state or "rogue nation" or jihadist terror organization has a comparable record of such massive murderous global aggression.

As rulers of the planet, US leaders are inclined to pursue *imperial diplomacy* rather than *traditional diplomacy*. Traditional diplomacy is that process of settling disputes by looking for workable compromises, finding solutions that might leave both sides less than completely satisfied, but satisfied enough to avoid armed conflict.

Imperial diplomacy is something else, something of an oxymoron. It usually begins with the issuance of a set of demands that are implicitly treated as nonnegotiable—even if presented as "proposals." The other side's resistance or even hesitancy to accede to US demands are denounced by Washington as an unwillingness to negotiate in good faith ("they are being uncooperative"). US leaders announce they are running out of patience—as if they had manifested any patience to begin with. If concessions are made by the weaker nation, the empire then escalates its demands. Despite the other side's attempts at accommodation and concession, in short time it is labeled as recalcitrant and belligerent and is subjected to US attack. Such was the pattern in regard to Iraq, Panama, Somalia, Nicaragua (under the Sandinistas), the Bosnian Serbs, Yugoslavia, and Iran, to name a few recent instances.

Imperial diplomacy is inclined to ignore treaties and international law, accepting only the limitations imposed by self-interest and power. Even the *New York Times,* seldom critical of US overseas initiatives, reported that people in many countries had "a widespread vision of America as an imperial power that has defied world opinion through unjustified and unilateral use of military force."[5]

Here is an incomplete list of unilateral and imperious diplomatic stances taken by the United States within a brief span of time (mostly in one year, 2001):

- December 1997: the Treaty to Ban Land Mines was signed by 122 nations. The United States refused to sign. *We don't use them.*
- July 1998: the International Criminal Court Treaty, to try political and military personnel charged with crimes against humanity, was approved by 120 countries. Washington opposed the treaty. In December 2001 the US Senate passed an amendment that would exempt American military personnel from complying with the jurisdiction of the new court.
- February 2001: the United States refused to join 123 nations pledged to ban the use and production of antipersonnel bombs and mines.
- March 2001: the Kyoto Protocol of 1997 (dealing with global warming), which the United States never signed, was declared "dead" by the White House.
- April 2001: the United States stood virtually alone in opposing UN resolutions acknowledging a human right to adequate food, a moratorium on the death penalty, and lower costs for HIV/AIDS drugs.
- May 2001: the United States refused to participate in international talks on ways to crack down on offshore and other tax and money-laundering havens.
- July 2001: the United States was the only nation to oppose the UN Agreement to Curb the International Flow of Illicit Small Arms.
- October 2001: the UN General Assembly passed a resolution, for the tenth consecutive year, calling for an end to the US embargo against Cuba, by a vote of 167 to 3 (the United States, Israel, and the Marshall Islands voted in opposition).
- November 2001: the United States forced a vote in the UN Committee on Disarmament and Security to demonstrate its opposition to the Comprehensive [Nuclear] Test Ban Treaty.

- December 2001: the United States officially withdrew from the Anti-ballistic Missile Treaty, renouncing a major arms control accord.[6]

Two-Party Imperialism

The powers of the plutocracy weigh heavily upon US foreign policy regardless of the personality or political party that occupies the White House. In 2008, when the Bush/Cheney reactionaries were replaced by the reputedly forward-looking Obama administration, it proved to be more a changing of the guard than a changing of policy.

President Obama made no dramatic cuts in military spending and actually raised the Pentagon's budget after taking office. He increased funding for the costly and bloody aggressions in Iraq and Afghanistan. By August 2010 he was claiming an end to the engagement in Iraq and supposedly had removed all combat units. But 50,000 US troops remained in that country, with an even larger number of privately contracted mercenaries whose presence kept growing as regular troops were withdrawn.[7] While the remaining US troops were no longer to engage in combat, they would continue to "fight terrorism" and were slated to stay for years to come. In addition, the door was left open for the eventual return of additional combat units should they be needed. Ending the war seemed to resemble continuing it.

Also overlooked was the fortress-like compound that the US continued to occupy in Iraq, the "green zone," reportedly the largest and most heavily fortified "diplomatic post" in the world, the size of Vatican City or some other mini-state, with its own rigorous security and defense perimeter, and its own self-contained energy and water systems—not exactly the embassy of a nation-state performing normal diplomatic tasks.

Meanwhile in Afghanistan, American forces were declared by Obama to be engaged in a "war of necessity"—supposedly to prevent another 9/11. But of the hundreds of thousands of people killed by US and NATO forces in Iraq and Afghanistan, not one has been identified as linked to the events of 9/11. According to one critic, the United States was drawn into Afghanistan to provide a stronger US presence in the oil-rich Persian Gulf and Caspian Sea region, and another military perch from which to bear down upon nearby Iran.[8] (It also has recently been announced that Afghanistan has vast and rich mineral deposits.)

Has the invasion of Afghanistan really prevented acts of terrorism? Has an occupational force in that country really made it impossible for any handful of terrorists to gather in a room, make plans, and plant bombs in heavily trafficked and congested areas of New York, Madrid, and London (all of which have been hit by terrorist attacks even after 9/11 and after the invasion of Afghanistan). Small groups of terrorists intent upon attacking unguarded civilian populations need to be hunted down and arrested by specially trained units before they can perform their murderous acts. But we do not defend against such threats by invading far-off countries, bombing whole villages, and killing large numbers of innocent people who have no link to any war of terror against the United States.

The empire expands its military reach in other areas. In 2010 Costa Rica, a nation whose constitution disallows any armed forces, agreed to having 7,000 US Marines within its territory and 46 US warships in its waters, along with 200 Black Hawk helicopters and other aircraft, thus augmenting the already substantial US military presence in Central America.

The previous year, Colombia signed a ten-year agreement permitting the United States to occupy seven military bases and all necessary civilian installations for the professed purpose of combating "the constant threat ... of anti-US governments in the region." The bases are to be endowed with "full spectrum military operations," meaning they would be capable of launching forces at full-scale levels of combat, including all-out war throughout South America. With this agreement, Washington deepened its ties to a Colombian military known for having the worst human rights record in Latin America, which is saying quite a lot.[9] (In August 2010, the Colombian Supreme Court ruled that the agreement could not come into force until it was approved by the Colombian Congress.[10])

President Obama gave an impression of charting a new course by declaring (when receiving the Nobel Peace Prize in 2009) that disarming America's nuclear arsenal would be a centerpiece of his foreign policy. But his budget the following year revealed an *increase* of $7 billion for the research and further development of nuclear weaponry, "the most money ever requested by an Administration for nuclear weapons."[11]

The country that receives the bulk of US foreign aid is Israel, a nation that defies classification as either satellite or enemy of the US imperium. Israel imposes a continually repressive policy of land incursions and colonization upon the Palestinian population in Gaza and the West Bank without incurring any restraints from Washington. It is said that in the Middle East, Israel plays a *subimperialism* role to the United States, acting as a "stabilizing force," a curb against revolutionary upheaval in the region. Debate continues among political writers as to whether it is the US or Israel that has the upper hand on Middle East policy. To be sure, with its well-financed Zionist lobbies and big-moneyed contributions to both Republicans and Democrats— unmatched by anything the anti-Zionists can muster—Israel exercises a most impressive influence over US policy in the region, an influence that extends into Congress, the State Department, and the White House itself, regardless of which party is in charge.[12]

Bleeding the Republic

As noted earlier, the empire feeds off the republic. Every year hundreds of billions of dollars, the lion's share of the discretionary budget, goes to the military to maintain its global web of bases, pursue its numerous wars, provide for its mercenary armies, and bolster its authoritarian satellite regimes.

We the people are sinking into ever harder times in order to sustain imperial dominion. In the United States we witness a skyrocketing military budget and national debt, the worst recession in decades, over a trillion dollar annual federal deficit—along with record profits for the Pentagon contractors and record profits for the Wall Street plutocracy. For 2011 President Obama budgeted $50 billion in foreign aid, twice the amount of the previous year. As noted earlier, foreign aid mostly aids corporate contractors and corrupt Third World vassals. Obama also doubled the US State Department budget to almost $52 billion, signaling an increase in interventionist initiatives.

Well into his presidency Obama and his national security state continued their direct and indirect involvement in various wars (Iraq, Afghanistan, northern Pakistan, Somalia, Yemen) while leveling military threats against Iran, Venezuela, and North Korea. In 2010, instead of sending medical and rescue aid to Haiti's earthquake victims (as did Cuba), Obama sent in 15,000 marines to keep order and make sure no insurgency might develop. This is the same US Marine Corps that engaged in years of repression and killings in Haiti decades ago and supported more recent massacres by proxy forces. At the same time, the president declared a freeze on all discretionary social spending and human services within the United States itself.

The immense cost of maintaining a global empire has left us with a republic in decline. The annual US trade deficit reached almost $50 billion by 2010. The United States was now the biggest debtor country in the world, with an accumulated debt of close to $15 trillion, much of it owed to China and other foreign governments. Basic domestic services were being eliminated by state and local governments that faced record insolvency. Federal allocations to states and municipalities were declining by 10 percent or more each year. Public hospitals were closing for lack of funds, libraries were reducing their hours, schools were being shut down, and teaching staffs were being cut. Medical costs continued to skyrocket. Public services for the very poor and disabled were being reduced; firefighters and police were being laid off. Meanwhile, the White House was considering cutbacks in Social Security and Medicare.[13]

The country's infrastructure was at risk, with water and sewage systems needing repair along with bridges, roads, tunnels, shorelines, levees, reservoirs, and public transportation. Aging mass transit systems lacked funds for maintenance, upgrades, and sufficient service even while more people were depending on them. In summer 2010, one city was trying to save funds by turning off a third of its lights, and a number of local governments were breaking up roads they could no longer afford to maintain, turning them into gravel.[14]

Inequality in income and wealth was increasing. Real wages were declining while homelessness grew. As of July 2010, upwards of 30 million Americans were out of work or seriously underemployed with only part-time jobs, with no sign of a dramatic turnaround. At least thirty-two states—unable to pay unemployment benefits to citizens in dire need—borrowed billions from a US Treasury that itself was trillions of dollars in debt. While hunger was growing amid the most destitute, Congress cut almost $12 billion from food stamps allocation.[15]

Impoverishment of the republic is seen as a bad thing by people who think that government should play a role in advancing social betterment. But the reactionaries seek to transform America into a

Third World nation, rolling back the social wage and bringing living standards more in line with the free market paradise of Indonesia. For them, drastic cutbacks in public spending and a decline in wages are just fine. Hence, the costs of empire serve a multifold purpose: assuring plutocratic supremacy abroad with a strong military, fat-profit contracts for corporate America, and defunding human services at home.

The republic is bled in another way: the empire continues to tighten its grip on our democratic rights. The statist psychology fostered by perpetual war makes democratic dissent difficult if not "unpatriotic" and provides an excuse to circumscribe our civil liberties, such as they are. Under newly enacted repressive legislation, almost any critical effort against existing policy can be defined as "giving aid and comfort to terrorism."[16]

After hardly two years in office, President Obama claimed the power to incarcerate individuals for life and execute US citizens without charges or due process. He adopted his predecessor's secret prisons and Patriot Act gag orders. He contrived new ways of denying habeas corpus. He granted complete legal immunity to officeholders who had committed serious crimes in the previous administration. His own administration operated without the transparency promised during the electoral campaign. Special operation forces were deployed in at least seventy-five countries by 2010, up from sixty the year before. "Obama has allowed things that the previous administration did not," claimed one official.[17]

As of 2011 the Obama administration was seeking authority from Congress to compel Internet service providers to make our Internet records available to government investigators. Under the pretense of fighting terrorism and espionage, security agencies would be able to track protestors and dissidents at will, undermining the Fourth Amendment of the US Constitution, which states that people have a right to be secure in their persons, houses, papers, and effects against unreasonable search and seizure.[18]

The Collapse of Empire?

Various writers seem to think that the American empire is in serious decline. There are signs to consider. As just observed, the American *economy* is in serious trouble, with chronic recession, structural unemployment, growing poverty, and a huge foreign debt and trade deficit.

In South America, countries like Venezuela, Bolivia, Ecuador, and Argentina are pursuing a reformist self-developing path in defiance of the imperial New World Order. Not only in South America but across the planet, opinion is largely critical of US arrogance and aggression.

Then there is the Colossus of the East: China. With its massive population and dramatic economic growth, China is out-producing just about everyone else, emerging as the most formidable player in the international economy, the only country that seems to have no fear of the United States. While the United States sinks deeper into debt, China grows in production and earnings. China also controls the credit and holds the chips.

Furthermore, as Andre Vltchek reports, China is developing impressively. The government is trying to introduce universal health insurance and more adequate environmental protections. Minimal wages are much higher than in Indonesia and the Philippines, and vastly better than in India. The present Beijing administration is re-introducing labor protection for workers. China has constructed the longest network of electric trains, running at over 400km/h (fastest in the world). More than thirty cities are building massive subway systems, while a dozen other cities already have such systems. The trains, buses, and subways charge modest fares, being themselves publicly subsidized. Public buses run on electricity or natural gas. Bicycle lanes are everywhere, and electric bicycles are being produced and encouraged. In addition, there are the admirable new public parks with lakes, sports facilities, and free exercise machines used by many.

And China is the only country in Asia that has a coherent population control program. With its one-child policy it is making a strong effort at "sustainability."[19]

Meanwhile, China is outperforming the US global empire. As James Petras points out, in parts of Latin America, Africa, and especially Asia, China is emerging as the principal trading partner. While the US wallows in pointless conflicts in marginal countries like Somalia, Yemen, and Afghanistan and organizes a dirty coup in tiny Honduras, "China signs on to billion-dollar joint ventures in oil and iron projects in Brazil and Venezuela and an Argentine grain production. The US specializes in propping up broken states like Mexico and Columbia, while China invests heavily in extractive industries in Angola, Nigeria, South Africa, and Iran" and "deepens its links with the dynamic economies of South Korea, Japan, Vietnam, Brazil, and the oil riches of Russia and the raw materials of Africa."[20]

Getting back to the United States: before predicting the fall of the US empire, we should not underestimate its capacity for durability and regeneration. Setbacks and defeats do not necessarily consign empires to the graveyard of history. The United States suffered a serious defeat in Vietnam, yet in the face of dire predictions to the contrary, US imperialism became still stronger in the years that followed.

An empire dedicated to boundless corporate plunder is—unfortunately—more likely to undo the global ecosphere before it undoes itself. The titanic expenditures needed to maintain military supremacy leave little money for environmental initiatives. Drought problems—once peculiar only to the US Southwest—now threaten every region of the country. Pollution and health problems intensify as chemical spraying over rural and urban communities increases. In the aftermath of America's worst environmental disaster (the BP oil spill in the Gulf of Mexico) President Obama did not reverse his endorsement of deepwater drilling and nuclear power. In his first two years in office, he did next to nothing about the climate crisis.

A secret Pentagon report from 2004 predicted that global catastrophe was imminent and perhaps even unavoidable. "Disruption and conflict will be endemic features of life."[21] In a Russia beset by drought and record temperatures, fires destroyed millions of acres of farmlands and forests in 2010, along with one-third of Russia's grain crop. Whole villages were destroyed. Thousands of people sickened from the smoke inhalation, and thousands died as carbon monoxide levels reached over six times the maximum allowable level. The death rate in Moscow doubled amid the heat and toxic smoke. In Pakistan that same year, nearly twenty million people lost everything to floods; over 1,500 perished.[22]

The US empire presides over the global unraveling of nature without so much as a plan of action. The US empire has more important things to do: pursue corporate profit opportunities and capital accumulation, and vanquish those who try to oppose or deviate from this course. To the extent the empire deals at all with the climate crisis, it is only to figure out new ways of making a profit off it.[23]

Thinking Outside the Paradigm

Contrary to the established myth that capitalism fosters democracy, the moneyed class has always opposed the broadening of popular rights and has shown itself hostile to any kind of democratic activism and working-class resistance to plutocracy.

Do not think your rulers are not interested in what you think. That is all they are interested in about you. They usually are not terribly concerned about your health, literacy, or well-being. But they are keenly interested in what might be stirring in your mind. The pictures in your head are of real concern to them. They conjure false issues to distract or flatter or frighten the populace, or in some other way win over or confuse people. They do all they can to manipulate the flow of information and disinformation. But they are not always successful. Sometimes reality is too much for them to cloak with their mendacity.

There sometimes are limits to how well officialdom and the corporate press can finesse reality. In both the Vietnam and Iraqi wars, US officials, along with a complicit press, could not totally get past the awful actuality of the war itself, the *reality principle* that sets limits on propaganda. Despite every manipulation and repeated assurances of impending success, the two wars became increasingly unpopular and politically costly.

Yet, to a large extent, the dominant paradigm has prevailed. The debate around the Vietnam and Iraq wars was limited to those who said that US forces could win and those who said they could not. There have been those of us who urged a different position. For us, the debate should center on the horrors of war and the lies with which war was justified, wars of imperialism fought hypocritically in the name of democracy. For us, regardless of whether these wars were "successful" or not, regardless of whether they could be won (whatever that meant) or not, they were unjust and harmful. In both cases, the military invasion with its unwarranted slaughter of civilian populations was a crime against humanity. In expenditures of treasure and blood, each was a war that violated the interests of both the American people and the people in those other countries. But we were never afforded a platform in the mainstream media to explore those enormous truths.

As with wars, so with domestic issues: the reality principle sometimes sets a limit on propaganda. When Republican leaders said we have the finest medical system in the world, millions of Americans who have no access to that system or who have been victimized by it in one way or another found it hard to believe such claims.

In other words (faithful viewers of Fox News to one side), indoctrination does not operate with perfect effect. In the face of all monopolistic ideological manipulation, people still develop a skepticism toward the official ideology. *Reality* is a problem for the ruling class. Reality has to be constantly finessed and misrepresented because *reality is radical.* There is a limit to how many lies people will swallow. Along with institutional stability we have popular ferment and popular innovation. Along with ruling class coercion we have skepticism and sometimes even mass resistance. All social institutions of capitalist society have a dichotomous tension within them. They must sustain the few while appearing to serve the many. And sometimes the many, beset and distracted as they are by so much else, do catch wise and resist. The empire is only as secure as the lies it can sell.

By becoming aware of this, we have a better chance of moving against the tide and resisting the deadening hand of free market plutocracy, a better chance of exposing the dominant imperial paradigm for the suffocating dirty little box that it really is, a better chance to build a real and viable democracy amid a family of nations in a peaceful and sustainable world.

Notes

Chapter 1

1. Carl Becker, *The Heavenly City of the Eighteenth Century Philosophers* (Yale University Press, 2003).

2. http://en.wikiquote.org/wiki/Upton_Sinclair.

3. See Michael Parenti, *The Assassination of Julius Caesar* (New Press, 2003).

4. *The Economist*, June 2003, www.timeenoughforlove.org/Politics.htm.

5. See the discussion regarding the Project for a New American Century in Michael Parenti, *Superpatriotism* (City Lights, 2004), 133–144.

6. Stephen Peter Rosen, "The Future of War and the American Military," *Harvard Magazine*, vol. 104, no. 5, 2002.

7. Chalmers Johnson, *The Sorrows of Empire* (Holt, 2005), and his *Nemesis: The Last Days of the American Republic* (Metropolitan Books, 2007).

8. For a very incomplete listing of recommended works, see James Petras, *Global Depression and Regional Wars* (Clarity Press, 2009); James Petras, *Rulers and Ruled in the US Empire* (Clarity Press, 2007); Eva Golinger, *The Empire's Web* (Monte Avila, 2009); Berch Berberoglu (ed.), *Globalization and Change* (Lexington Books, 2005); Gregory Elich, *Strange Liberators* (Llumina Press, 2006); Gerald Horne, *Blows Against the Empire* (International Publishers, 2008); Henry Veltmeyer, *Globalization and Antiglobalization* (Ashgate, 2005); Francis Robert Shor, *Dying Empire* (Routledge, 2010); and David Harvey, *The New Imperialism* (Oxford University Press, 2005).

9. For some other examples of these shallow critiques, along with Chalmers Johnson, consider Stephen Kinzer, *Overthrow: America's Century of Régime*

Change from Hawaii to Iraq (Henry Holt, 2006); Michael Hunt, *The American Ascendancy* (University of North Carolina Press, 2008); Peter Beinart, *The Icarus Syndrome: A History of American Hubris* (Harper, 2010); Andrew Bacevich, *Washington Rules: America's Path to Permanent War* (Metropolitan Books, 2010); Clifford Krauss, *Inside Central America* (Summit Books, 1991); and William Pfaff, *The Irony of Manifest Destiny* (Walker, 2010).

10. For some basic studies, see L. S. Stavrianos, *Global Rift* (William Morrow, 1981); Claude Ake, *A Political Economy of Africa* (Longman, 1981); and the bitterly poetic Eduardo Galeano, *Open Veins of Latin America* (Monthly Review Press, 1997).

11. Donald McNeil Jr., "The Curse of Plenty," *New York Times,* 20 June 2010.

12. For a few horrendous examples of imperial carnage, see Mike Davis, *Late Victorian Holocausts* (Verso, 2001); Carl Boggs, *The Crimes of Empire* (Pluto Press, 2010); Jon M. Bridgman, *The Revolt of the Hereros* (University of California Press, 1981).

13. *New York Times,* 30 November 1992.

14. For details, see Michael Parenti, "Defying the Sanctions: A Flight to Iraq," *North Coast Express,* Spring 2001.

Chapter 2

1. Paul Street, "Obama's Violin," *Z Magazine,* May 2009.

2. However with the deep recession of 2008–2011 and no sign of major recovery in sight, the Social Security fund's surplus was shrinking; see Justin Fox's report, 9 April 2009: time.com/time/business/article/0,8599,1890542,00 .html.

3. Bill Quigley, "Corporations Profit from Permanent War, " 28 May 2010, ZNet Daily Commentary.

4. See various issues of *The Defense Monitor,* newsletter of the Center for Defense Information, vol. 39.

5. *New York Times,* 22 August 2010; Bill Quigley, "Corporations Profit from Permanent War, " 28 May 2010, ZNet Daily Commentary.

6. Winslow Wheeler, "Nightmare Budget Scenarios at the Pentagon," *Defense Monitor,* April/May/June 2010.

7. Thorstein Veblen, *The Theory of the Business Enterprise* (Charles Scribner's Sons, 1932), 217.

8. Gareth Smyth and Thomas Catan, "UN Auditors Attack US Occupiers over Spending of Iraq's Oil Revenues," *Financial Times*, 22 June 2004; James Surowiecki, "Army Inc.," *New Yorker*, 12 January 2004; David R. Baker, "Rebuilding Iraq a Lucrative Job," *San Francisco Chronicle*, 21 March 2004; *New York Times*, 26 July 2007.

9. David Armstrong, "Dick Cheney's Song of America: Drafting a Plan for Global Dominance," *Harper's Magazine*, October 2002. The plan went through several drafts with titles like *Defense Planning Guidance for the 1994–1999 Fiscal Years* and *Defense Planning Guidance for the 2004–2009 Fiscal Years*.

10. See Catherine Lutz (ed.), *The Bases of Empire* (NYU Press, 2009).

11. *Washington Post*, 4 May 2010.

12. Rachel Stohl and Rhea Myerscough, "In the Name of Fighting Terrorism, The United States Is Still Arming the World," *Defense Monitor*, September/October 2006; also http://useconomy.about.com/od/usfederalbudget/p/military_budget.htm.

13. *New York Times*, 23 April 2010.

14. See John Lasker, "US Space Weapon Now Circling the Globe," *Toward Freedom*, 27 May 2010, http://towardfreedom.com/home/content/view/1980/1/.

15. The quoted phrases are from "No Place for Jingoism," *New York Times*, editorial, 4 July 2010.

16. Mark Landler, reporting in *New York Times*, 23 April 2010.

17. For evidence in support of this see Michael Parenti, *Against Empire* (City Lights, 1995); Michael Parenti, *Inventing Reality*, 2nd ed. (Wadsworth/Thomson, 1993); and the writings of James Petras, William Blum, and various others.

18. Carl Boggs and Tom Pollard, *The Hollywood War Machine: US Militarism and Popular Culture* (Paradigm, 2006); and Nick Turse, *The Complex: How the Military Invades Our Everyday Lives* (Holt, 2009).

19. Andrew Alexander, "The Soviet Threat Was a Myth," www.buzzle.com, 18 April 2002.

20. On the destruction of Yugoslavia, see Chapter 9.

21. *San Francisco Chronicle* editorial, 15 February 1998.

22. Robert Scheer, "An Illusion of Terror," *San Francisco Chronicle,* 12 January 2005.

23. Robert Dreyfuss, *Devil's Game: How the United States Helped Unleash Fundamentalist Islam* (Metropolitan Books/Henry Holt, 2005).

24. See the discussion in Michael Parenti, *Superpatriotism* (City Lights, 2004), 145–150.

Chapter 3

1. See Robert Gaylon Ross Sr., *Who's Who of the Elite: Members of the Bilderbergs, Council on Foreign Relations, & Trilateral Commission,* rev. ed. (RIE, 2000); Laurence Shoup and William Minter, *Imperial Brain Trust: The Council on Foreign Relations and United States Foreign Policy* (Authors Choice Press, 2004); Daniel Estulin, *The True Story of the Bilderberg Group,* 2nd ed. (Trine Day, 2009); Howard Wiarda, *Conservative Brain Trust* (Lexington Books, 2008); Leslie Sklair, *The Transnational Capitalist Class* (Blackwell, 2001); Armand Santilli, *The Boys at Bohemian Grove* (Xlibris Corporation, 2004).

2. See Ingo Muller, *Hitler's Justice* (Harvard University Press, 1991), part 3, "The Aftermath."

3. Jon Wiener, "Bringing Nazi Sympathizers to the US," *Nation,* 6 March 1989.

4. Herbert Lottman, *The Purge* (William Morrow, 1986), 290.

5. Hugh Deane, "Korea, China, and the United States: A Look Back," *Monthly Review,* February 1995. On the struggle for democracy in South Korea, see Georgy Katsiaficas and Na Kahn-chae, *South Korean Democracy* (Routledge, 2006).

6. Roy Palmer Domenico, *Italian Fascists on Trial, 1943–1948* (University of North Carolina Press, 1991), passim.

7. *La Repubblica,* 9 April 1995; *Corriere della Sera,* 27 and 28 March 1995, 12 April 1995, and 29 May 1995; see also Jonathan Kwitney, "The CIA's Secret Armies in Europe," *Nation,* 6 April 1992.

8. H. Keith Melton and Robert Wallace, *The Official CIA Manual of Trickery and Deception* (William Morrow, 2009); Trevor Paglen, *Blank Spots on the Map: The Dark Geography of the Pentagon's Secret World* (Dutton, 2009); Javier Giraldo, S. J., *Columbia: The Genocidal Democracy* (Common Courage,

1996); Horacio Verbitsky, *The Flight: Confessions of an Argentine Dirty Warrior* (New Press, 1996); Peter Dale Scott, *American War Machine* (Rowman and Littlefield, 2010); David McGowan, *Derailing Democracy* (Common Courage, 2000); Daniel Estulin, *Shadow Masters*, 2nd ed. (Common Courage, 2008); John Perkins, *Confessions of an Economic Hit Man* (Berrett-Koehler, 2004); Frances Stonor Saunders, *The Cultural Cold War: The CIA and the World of Arts and Letters* (New Press, 2001); Reed Brody, *Contra Terror in Nicaragua* (South End Press, 1985); Holly Sklar, *Washington's War on Nicaragua* (South End Press, 1989).

9. See John Quigley, *The Ruses for War: American Intervention Since World War II* (Prometheus Books, 1992); and William Blum, *Killing Hope: US Military and CIA Interventions Since World War II*, updated (Common Courage, 2008).

10. Blum, *Killing Hope*, passim.

11. For a more detailed account on Iraq, see Chapter 9.

12. Quoted in Carl Oglesby, *Ravens in the Storm* (Scribner, 2008), 120.

Chapter 4

1. Peter Gowan, "The NATO Powers and the Balkan Tragedy," *New Left Review*, March-April 1999, 103–104.

2. By "free market," of course, we are referring to the investment processes related to global neoliberal corporate domination, which are neither free nor a market.

3. James Petras, *Rulers and Ruled in the US Empire* (Clarity Press, 2007), 89.

4. Petras, *Rulers and Ruled in the US Empire*, 89.

5. Michael Parenti, *Blackshirts and Reds: Rational Fascism and the Overthrow of Communism* (City Lights, 1997), chapters 6 and 7.

6. News report, KQED-NPR, 31 May 2010.

7. Michael Parenti, "Free Market 'Reform' and Communism's Suppression," *Peace Review*, vol. 9, no. 1 (1997); Vladimire Bilenkin, "Russian Workers Under the Yeltsin Regime: Notes on a Class in Defeat," *Monthly Review*, November 1996.

8. *New York Times*, 18 August 2001; and report by former head of the West German Secret Service Hans Geoirge-Wieck in *La Libre Belgique*, 31

August 2001; M. Raphael Johnson, "European Nationalist a Victim of US Intelligence Smears," *American Free Press,* 13 October 2003.

9. *New York Times,* 6 to 20 November 1983; and Daniel Lazare, "Reagan's Seven Big Lies About Grenada," *In These Times,* 6 November 1983.

10. "A Tottering Structure of Lies," *Sojourner,* December 1983; and Michael Massing, "Grenada Before and After," *Atlantic Monthly,* February 1984.

11. See "Special Report," *Labor Action* (publication of the Labor Coalition on Central America, Washington, DC), July/August 1990; Clarence Lusane, "Aftermath of the US Invasion," *CovertAction Information Bulletin,* Spring 1991.

12. *New York Times,* 3 February 1953.

13. Quoted in Richard Barnet, "The Uses of Force," *New Yorker,* 29 April 1991, 90.

14. When the text of Clinton's speech was printed the next day in the *New York Times,* the sentence quoted above was omitted.

15. *New York Times,* 5 October 1993. For a full account of Yeltsin's repression, see my "Yeltsin's Coup and the Media's Alchemy," in Michael Parenti, *Dirty Truths* (City Lights, 1996), 133–140.

16. Samuel P. Huntington, "Why International Primacy Matters," *International Security* 17 (Spring 1993), 82–83.

17. Quoted in Gordon Laxer, "Radical Transformative Nationalisms Confront the US Empire," *Current Sociology,* vol. 51, no. 2 (March 2003).

18. Both OPIC and USAID statements in Gregory Elich, "The CIA's Covert War," *CovertAction Quarterly,* April-June 2001.

19. *Financial Times,* 11 April 2001. The number of companies slated for privatization was actually 4,500 in April but grew to over 7,000 by July 2001, according to a communication to me from Barry Lituchy, editor of *Eastern European Review.*

20. Jonathan Marshall, Peter Dale Scott, and Jane Hunter, *The Iran-Contra Connection* (South End, 1988); *Report of the Congressional Committee Investigating the Iran-Contra Affair* (Government Printing Office, 1987).

21. See Frank Rich, *The Greatest Story Ever Sold: The Decline and Fall of Truth in Bush's America* (Penguin, 2007); and John Dean, *Worse Than Watergate: The Secret Presidency of George W. Bush* (Warner Books, 2005).

22. Christopher Hitchens, *The Trial of Henry Kissinger* (London: Verso, 2001), 98–99.

23. See Information Security Oversight Office, *Report to the President* (National Archives and Records Administration, 2009).

24. Cable of 16 October 1970, quoted in Hitchens, *The Trial of Henry Kissinger*, 60.

25. See Daniel Ellsberg, "Lying About Vietnam," *New York Times*, 29 June 2001.

Chapter 5

1. See, for example, Walter Rodney, *How Europe Underdeveloped Africa*, rev. ed. (Howard University Press, 1981); and Eduardo Galeano, *Open Veins of Latin America: Five Centuries of the Pillage of a Continent* (Monthly Review Press, 1997).

2. Michael Parenti, *Against Empire* (City Lights Books, 1995), 8. For an overview of past and present global development, see Ha-Joon Chang, *Bad Samaritans: The Myth of Free Trade and the Secret History of Capitalism* (Bloomsbury Press, 2008).

3. Christopher Cook, *Diet for a Dead Planet* (New Press, 2004), 229–238.

4. Oxfam International, "A Raw Deal for Rice Under DR-CAFTA," 16 November 2004.

5. Jonathan M. Katz, "With Cheap Food Imports, Haiti Can't Feed Itself," www.huffingtonpost.com/2010/03/20/with-cheap-food-imports -h_n_507228.html.

6. Kevin Edmunds, "Empty Promises and Empty Bellies: Bill Clinton's Doubletalk on Haitian Agriculture," 17 May 2010, https://nacla .org/.

7. Norm Dixon, "G8: How the Rich World Short-Changes Africa," *Green Left Weekly*, 6 July 2005; Marc Lacy, "Africans' Burden: West's Farm Subsidies," *New York Times*, 10 September 2003.

8. For an overview, see Amy Chua, *World on Fire: How Exporting Free Market Democracy Breeds Ethnic Hatred and Global Instability* (Doubleday, 2003).

9. "Child Labor," UNICEF report, updated 6 March 2008, www.unicef .org/protection/index_childlabour.html.

10. Graham Hancock, *Lords of Poverty: The Power, Prestige, and Corruption of the International Aid Business* (Atlantic Monthly Press, 1989).

11. James Ridgeway, "Bay of Piglets," *Village Voice*, 15 December 1992.

12. See Ngaire Woods, *The Globalizers: The IMF, the World Bank, and Their Borrowers* (Cornell University Press, 2007); and Richard Peet, *Unholy Trinity: The IMF, World Bank, and WTO*, 2nd ed. (Zed Books, 2009).

Chapter 6

1. On NAFTA, see Jeff Faux, *The Global Class War* (Wiley, 2006).

2. See Lori Wallach and Michelle Sforza, *The WTO* (Seven Stories Press, 2000); and John R. MacArthur, *The Selling of Free Trade: NAFTA, Washington, and the Subversion of American Democracy* (Hill and Wang, 2000).

3. On the examples given in the last two paragraphs above, see *New York Times*, 30 April 1996 and 9 May 1997; and *Washington Post*, 13 October 1998.

4. The decade-long legal battle was fought not by the Indian government but by three women—Vandana Shiva, Magda Aelvoet, and Linda Bullard—and their ecologically minded organizations. See "EPO Revokes Neem Patent Rights," 10 March 2005, www.financialexpress.com/news/EPO% 20revokes%20neem%20patent%20rights/127729/.

5. Project Censored, "Real News," April 2007; also Arun Shrivastava, "Genetically Modified Seeds: Women in India Take on Monsanto," *Global Research*, 9 October 2006.

6. Vikas Bajaj, "In India, Walmart Goes to the Farm," *New York Times*, 12 April 2010.

7. Quoted in *People's Weekly World*, 7 December 1996.

8. Vandana Shiva, "Monsanto's Billion-Dollar Water Monopoly Plans," *Canadian Dimension*, February 2000; Malcolm McDowell, Maude Barlow, et al., *Blue Gold: World Water Wars* (DVD), 2009, directed by Sam Bozzo; and Wes Enzinna, "GWOT: El Salvador," *Nation*, 31 December 2007.

9. "The Codex Committee on Food Labeling Meets in Quebec," *Common Man News*, 17 May 2010, http://themancommon.blogspot.com/2010/05/codex-committee-on-food-labeling-meets.html.

10. See Clive George, *The Truth About Trade* (Zed Books, 2010).

11. John R. MacArthur, *The Selling of "Free Trade": NAFTA, Washington, and the Subversion of American* Democracy (Hill & Wang, 2000); and Sarah Anderson and John Cavanagh, "NAFTA's Unhappy Anniversary," *New York Times*, 7 February 1995.

12. For a detailed discussion, see Steven Shrybman, "Memorandum: United Parcel Service (UPS) v. Canada," 27 June 2007, www.cupw.ca/index.cfm/ci_id/9654/la_id/1.htm.

13. Kimberly Amadeo, "Disadvantages of NAFTA," About.com, 21 December 2009, http://useconomy.about.com/od/tradepolicy/p/NAFTA_Problems .htm.

14. Bruce Campbell, Carlos Salas, and Robert E. Scott, "NAFTA at Seven: Its Impact on Workers in All Three Nations," Economic Policy Institute, 31 March 2001.

15. Norm Nixon, "G8: How the Rich World Short-Changes Africa," *Green Left Weekly*, 6 July 2005.

16. Paul Krugman, "The Pain Caucus," *New York Times*, 31 May 2010; and Chris Isidore, "Say Goodbye to Full-time Jobs with Benefits," 1 June 2010, http://money.cnn.com/2010/06/01/news/economy/contract_jobs/.

17. See Steven Shrybman, *A Citizen's Guide to the World Trade Organization* (Canadian Center for Policy Alternatives, 1999); and Ian Fletcher and Robert Luttwak, *Free Trade Doesn't Work* (US Business and Industry Council, 2010).

18. "US Seeks 'Get-Out Clause' for Illegal Farm Payments," Oxfam, 29 June 2006, www.oxfam.org/en/news/pressreleases2006/pr060629_wto_geneva.

19. "Oxfam Reaction to WTO Judgment on US Cotton Subsidies," 31 August 2009, www.oxfamamerica.org/press/pressreleases/oxfam-reaction -to-wto-judgment-on-us-cotton-subsidies.

20. Anthony Coughlin, correspondence to me, 24 January 2010. Coughlin has written widely about the darker side of the European Union.

Chapter 7

1. John Gerassi, letter to me, 30 June 2009. For an early overall view of social injustice in Latin America, see Gerassi's *The Great Fear in Latin America* (Collier Macmillan, 1965).

2. Andre Vltchek, correspondence to me, October 2010.

3. Gregory Elich, "Free Trade Disaster," *Correo del Orinoco*, 9 April 2010.

4. Elich, "Free Trade Disaster."

5. Elich, "Free Trade Disaster."

6. Elich, "Free Trade Disaster."

7. Elich, "Free Trade Disaster."

8. Elich, "Free Trade Disaster." For an excellent overview of the earlier colonial and postcolonial maldevelopment of Africa, see Claude Ake, *A Political Economy of Africa* (Longman, 1981).

9. Gregory Elich, "The Mean Heart of Capitalism," *Correo del Orinoco International* (Caracas), 4 June 2010.

10. Elich, "The Mean Heart of Capitalism."

11. Elich, "The Mean Heart of Capitalism."

12. Elich, "The Mean Heart of Capitalism"; for a more comprehensive study, see Gregory Elich, *Strange Liberators: Militarism, Mayhem, and the Pursuit of Profit* (Llumina Press, 2006).

13. Deidre Griswold, *Indonesia: The Second Greatest Crime of the Century* (World View, 1970).

14. Andre Vltchek, " Indonesia After Suharto," ZNet, April 2008, www .zcommunications.org/indonesia-after-shuarto-by-andre-vltchek.

15. According to documents released by the National Security Archive, www.gwu.edu/~nsarchiv/NSAEBB/NSAEBB176/index.htm, 24 January 2006; also John G. Taylor, *Indonesia's Forgotten War: The Hidden History of East Timor* (Zed Books/Pluto Press, 1991).

16. Vltchek, "Indonesia After Suharto." For a more comprehensive overview of the South Pacific region, see Andre Vltchek, *Oceania* (lulu press, 2010); also Commission for Reception, Truth, and Reconciliation in East Timor, Benetech Human Rights Data Analysis Group, 9 February 2006.

17. Vltchek, "Indonesia After Suharto."

18. Atmarita, "Nutrition Problems in Indonesia," Ministry of Health report, 19–20 March 2005, www.gizi.net/download/nutrition%20problem%20in% 20Indonesia.pdf.

19. Vltchek, "Indonesia After Suharto."

20. Vltchek, "Indonesia: Natural Disasters or Mass Murder?" n.d. (circa 2007), http://japanfocus.org/-Andre-Vltchek/2324; and Melinda Misuraca, communication to me, June 2010.

21. Vltchek, "Indonesia: Natural Disasters or Mass Murder?"

22. Vltchek, "Indonesia After Suharto."

23. Vltchek, "Indonesia After Suharto."

24. Vltchek, "Indonesia After Suharto."

25. Quoted in John Wojcik, "Kyrgyzstan: A 'Free Market' Disaster," *Political Affairs*, 9 April 2010, www.peoplesworld.org/kyrgyzstan-a-free-market-disaster.

26. Most of the above data are from Wojcik, "Kyrgyzstan: A 'Free Market' Disaster." Wojcik cites Mark Ames of the Moscow-based alternative newspaper *The Exile* for some of the information presented here; see also Elsa Claro, "Kyrgyzstan, The Faces of Eve," *International* (Havana), 24 June 2010.

27. Ames, cited in Wojcik, "Kyrgyzstan: A 'Free Market' Disaster"; Claro, "Kyrgyzstan, The Faces of Eve"; and *New York Times*, 8 June and 15 July 2010.

28. Claro, "Kyrgyzstan, The Faces of Eve."

Chapter 8

1. William Langer, *An Encyclopedia of World History*, 5th ed. (Houghton Mifflin, 1972), 1245–1248.

2. Granma International Online, "Cuba Notes 50th Anniversary of US Declaration of Unilateral War," Havana, Cuba, 19 March 2010, www.granma.cu/ingles/2010/text.htm.

3. Granma International Online, "Cuba Notes 50th Anniversary of US Declaration of Unilateral War."

4. Quoted in William Langer, *An Encyclopedia of World History*, 1246.

5. Morris Morley, *Imperial State and Revolution: The United States and Cuba, 1952–1986* (Cambridge University Press, 1987), 52–86; and CIA Memorandum, 12 November 1962, cited in Piero Gleijeses, *Conflicting Missions* (North Carolina University Press, 2002), 16.

6. Varona quoted in *New York Daily News*, 8 January 1961.

7. Robert Cirino, *Power to Persuade* (Bantam, 1974); also Victor Bernstein and Jesse Gordon, "The Press and the Bay of Pigs," Columbia University Forum reprint, Fall 1967.

8. *New York Times*, 8 January 1961; *Time*, 13 January 1961.

9. *New York Times*, 8 January 1961.

10. Center for Cuban Studies *Newsletter*, winter 1976.

11. *New York Times*, 1 August 1984.

12. "Raul Castro Chosen as Cuba's New President," CNN.com/world, 24 February 2008.

13. Bill McKibben, "The Cuba Diet," *Harper's Magazine*, April 2005; Hugh Warwick, "Cuba's Organic Revolution," *Third World Resurgence*, Issue #118–119 (Spring 2000).

14. US Interest Section memorandum H18422693-4, procured and quoted by Margot Pepper in her *Through the Wall, A Year in Havana* (Freedom Voices, 2005), 300.

15. Peter Kornbluh, "Luis Posada Carriles, the Declassified Record," *National Security Archive* (Electronic Briefing Book No. 153), 10 May 2005. Orlando Bosch's terrorist activities are fully documented by a Senate investigation led by Senator John Kerry into the activities of the CIA, and summarized in Warren Hinkle and William Turner, *Deadly Secrets* (Thunder Mouth Press, 1993).

16. Cheryl LaBash, "US Keeps Cuba in Imperialism's Crosshairs," *Workers World*, 15 January 2010; see also www.freethefive.org/. The Cuban Five, as they have become known, are Gerardo Hernández, Antonio Guerrero, Ramón Labañino, Fernando González, and René González.

17. Michael Parenti and Alicia Jrapko, "The Cuban Five and US Terrorism," *The Cuban Nation*, 12 December 2006.

Chapter 9

1. Sean Gervasi, "Germany and the Yugoslav Crisis," *CovertAction Quarterly* (Winter 1992–93), 41–42; Michel Chossudovsky, "Dismantling Former Yugoslavia, Recolonizing Bosnia," *CovertAction Quarterly* (Spring 1996); and Michel Chossudovsky, "Banking on the Balkans," THIS, July-August 1999.

2. *Interim Agreement for Peace and Self-government in Kosovo* (the "Rambouillet Agreement"), 23 February 1999, reproduced in full in *The Kosovo Dossier*, 2nd ed. (Lord Byron Foundation for Balkan Studies, 1999).

3. Michael Parenti, *To Kill a Nation: The Attack on Yugoslavia* (Verso, 2000), 119–124.

4. Kenny's comment made at a teach-in, Leo Baeck Temple, Los Angeles, 23 May 1999.

5. Parenti, *To Kill a Nation*, 130–163.

6. For example, see Mira Marković, *Night and Day, A Diary* (Dragiša Nikolić, 1995).

7. For instance, Raymond Bonner, "War Crimes Panel Finds Croat Troops 'Cleansed' the Serbs," *New York Times*, 21 March 1999, a revealing report by a reputable correspondent that was largely ignored.

8. John Ranz, paid advertisement, *New York Times*, 29 April 1993.

9. Neil Clark, "The Milošević Trial Is a Travesty," *Guardian*, 12 February 2004.

10. Gregory Elich, "The CIA's Covert War," *CovertAction Quarterly* (April–June 2001), 35–36.

11. Elich, "The CIA's Covert War," 38–39.

12. *Financial Times*, 11 April 2001; and a communication to me from Barry Lituchy, editor of *Eastern European Review*.

13. *San Francisco Chronicle*, 5 May 1999.

14. For an overview of the delusions about Yugoslav war, see Parenti, *To Kill a Nation*.

15. *San Francisco Chronicle*, 20 September 2002; and the testimony of former top terrorism expert under Bush, Richard Clarke, *60 Minutes*, CBS-TV, 21 March 2004.

16. *New York Times*, 24 January 2003.

17. John King, "Arming Iraq: A Chronology of U.S. Involvement," www.iranchamber.com/history/articles/arming_iraq.php, March 2003.

18. A Googling of "Saddam and Hitler" produces over 6,000 entries.

19. *Wall Street Journal*, 9 April 2003.

20. See the report *Rebuilding America's Defenses* promulgated by Project for a New American Century, the right-wing think tank whence came the top policymakers of the Bush Jr. administration.

21. See Robert Collier's reports in *San Francisco Chronicle*, 9 and 12 April 2003.

22. Susan Webb, "US Military Attacks Iraqi Unions," *People's Weekly World*, 13–19 December 2003.

23. Raymond Baker, Shereen Ismael, and Tareq Ismael (eds.), *Cultural Cleansing in Iraq* (Pluto Press, 2010).

24. Joshua Blakeney, "The Cancer at the Heart of the Propaganda Machine," *Canadian Dimension*, 9 August 2010, http://canadiandimension.com/articles/3253; and Max Fuller, "Ghosts of Jadiriyah," 14 November 2006, www.brusselstribunal.org/FullerJadiriyah.htm.

25. Andrew Quadri, "Military Action in Iraq Motivated by Money," www.ucsdguardian.org/cgi-bin/print?param=opinion_2003_.

26. Larry Everest, *Oil, Power & Empire: Iraq and the US Global Agenda* (Common Courage, 2004); and Yahya Sadowski, "No War for Whose Oil?" *Le Monde Diplomatique*, April 2003.

27. *San Francisco Chronicle*, 22 February 1998; see also London *Financial Times*, 24 February 1998.

28. Pratap Chatterjee, *Iraq, Inc.: A Profitable Occupation* (Seven Stories Press, 2004); Robert Scheer, "Profiting at Taxpayer Expense," *San Francisco Chronicle*, 27 June 2007; Charlie Cray, "Meet the War Profiteers," *Multinational Monitor*, November/December 2006.

29. Project for a New American Century, *Rebuilding America's Defenses*, www.informationclearinghouse.info/article3249.htm; James Petras, *The Power of Israel in the United States* (Clarity Press and Fernwood Books, 2006), 61–62 and passim; Patrick Seale, "A Costly Friendship," *Nation*, 21 July 2003.

30. William Blum, *The Anti-Empire Report*, 1 September 2010, www.killinghope.org.

31. *New York Times*, 3 June 2009.

32. Sharon LaFraniere, "Hidden Misery: A Glimpse into North Korea," *New York Times*, 10 June 2010.

33. For an informative overview, see Bruce Cumings, *The Korean War* (Modern Library, 2010).

34. See the discussion in Michael Parenti, *The Terrorism Trap* (City Lights, 2002), 2–3.

35. Cheney quoted in John Pilger, "The Real Story Behind America's War," *New Statesman*, 17 December 2001.

36. For instance, see *New York Times*, 25 July 2010.

37. Clinton and Gates quoted in *San Francisco Chronicle*, 31 May 2009. Obama quoted in "Obama Says North Korea Engaged in 'Belligerent' Behavior," *Bloomberg Business Week*, 27 June 2010.

38. *New York Times,* 8 June 2009.

39. Paul Sack, correspondence, *New York Times,* 27 May 2009.

40. *Washington Post,* 21 January 2005; *New York Times,* 11 May 2007.

41. See Seymour Hersh's report in *New Yorker,* 7 July 2008.

42. *New York Times,* 29 July 2010.

43. See Paul Craig Roberts in *CounterPunch,* 19–21 June 2009; and Seymour Hersh's report in *New Yorker,* 29 June 2008.

44. Russia Today, "USA Israel Can Destroy 10,000 Targets in Iran," 17 March 2010, www.youtube.com/watch?v=SD1usEplSCQ.

45. Noam Chomsky, "The Iranian Threat," *ZCommunications,* 28 June 2010.

46. Joshua Blakeney, "The Cancer at the Heart of the Propaganda Machine."

47. President Obama, Cairo speech, 4 June 2009, www.whitehouse.gov/the_press_office/Remarks-by-the-President-at-Cairo-University-6-04-09/.

48. See the comments by Manuel Garcia Jr., "Fearful Pride (North Korea's Second Nuclear Test)," 26 May 2009, www.counterpunch.org/garcia05262009.html.

49. Most of the information regarding Chávez's programs can be found in various editions of *Correo del Orinoco* International (English ed.), 2010, edited by Eva Golinger. For an overview of Chávez's achievements, see Michel Collon, *Les 7 Péchés d'Hugo Chávez* (Investig'Action, Couleur livres, 2009).

50. Simon Romero, "Venezuela Groups Get US Aid Amid Meddling Charges," *New York Times,* 9 November 2006; Eva Golinger, *Bush vs. Chávez: La Guerra de Washington contra Venezuela* (Editorial Jose Marti, 2006).

51. See, respectively, *San Francisco Chronicle,* 30 November 2001; *Financial Times,* 12 January 2002; and *The Nation,* 6 May 2002.

52. See Gregory Wilpert (ed.), *Coup Against Chávez in Venezuela: The Best International Reports of What Really Happened* (Fundación por Un Mondo Multipolar, 2003).

53. "Venezuelan Court Rules Against Dissident," *New York Times,* 16 April 2005.

54. Andre Vltchek, correspondence to me, October 2010.

55. *San Francisco Chronicle,* 18 April 2002.

56. *New York Times,* 5 April 2006.

Chapter 10

1. "Advance Global Human Security," FCNL Washington Newsletter, July/August 2003.

2. See Larry Elliott, "The Lost Decade," *Guardian*, 9 July 2003, for a survey of the decline in global living standards.

3. See Fred Goldstein, *Low-Wage Capitalism* (World View Forum, 2009), 3–10.

4. Gordon Laxer, "Radical Transformative Nationalisms Confront the US Empire," *Current Sociology*, vol. 51, no. 2 (March 2003).

5. *New York Times*, 11 September 2003.

6. Items researched by Richard Du Boff, Center for Research on Globalization, www.globalresearch.ca/articles/DUB112B.html.

7. Jeremy Scahill, "Iraq Withdrawal? Obama and Clinton Expanding US Paramilitary Force in Iraq," *Nation*, 22 July 2010.

8. Blum, *Anti-Empire Report*, 4 August 2010, http://killinghope.org/bblum6/aer84.htm/.

9. Eva Golinger, "Venezuela Will Suspend All Oil Shipments to the US in the Event of an Attack," 25 July 2010, www.Chavezcode.com/2010/07/update-venezuela-will-suspend-all-oil.html; and Diane Lefer and Hector Aristizábal, "Seven Bases in Colombia," *Presente!* Spring 2010.

10. "Colombian Court Suspends US Military Base Deal," Reuters, 17 August 2010, www.reuters.com/article/idUSN17163883.

11. Rebecca Riley, "Barack Obama's Nuclear Rhetoric," *Z Magazine*, June 2010.

12. James Petras, *The Power of Israel in the United States* (Clarity Press, 2006).

13. Leilani Dowell, "Imperialism at Home and Abroad," *Workers World*, http://blip.tv/file/3932564; *New York Times*, 27 July 2010.

14. *New York Times*, 13 and 25 July 2010, and 9 August 2010; *Financial Times*, 18 August 2010.

15. Bob Herbert, "The Horror Show," *New York Times*, 10 August 2010; Kathy Durkin, "Congress Cuts Billions from Food Stamps," *Workers World*, 22 August 2010.

16. See *New York Times* editorial, 28 September 2006.

17. *Washington Post*, 4 June 2010; Glenn Greenwald, "Robt Gibbs Attacks the Fringe Losers on the Left," *Salon*, 10 Aug 2010, www.salon.com/news/opinion/glenn_greenwald/2010/08/10/gibbs.

18. Tom Burghardt, "Big Brother: Obama Demands Access to Internet Records, in Secret and Without Court Review," *Global Research*, 13 August 2010, www.globalresearch.cu/index_php?context=va&aid=20599.

19. Andre Vltchek, correspondence to me, October 2010.

20. James Petras, "Imperialism and Imperial Barbarism," unpublished paper, September 2010.

21. Mark Townsend and Paul Harris, "Now the Pentagon Tells Bush: Climate Change Will Destroy Us," *The Observer*, 22 February 2004.

22. "Fallout from Russia's Fires," *Time*, 19 August 2010; "Pakistan Floods," *New York Times*, 27 August 2010, http://topics.nytimes.com/top/reference/timestopics/subjects/f/floods/2010_pakistan_floods/index.html.

23. Clive Thompson, "Disaster Capitalism," *Mother Jones*, July/August 2010.

Index

About the Author

Michael Parenti (Ph.D., Yale University) is an internationally known, award-winning author, scholar, and lecturer who addresses a wide variety of political and cultural subjects. Among his recent books are *God and His Demons* (2010), *Contrary Notions: The Michael Parenti Reader* (2007), *The Culture Struggle* (2006), *The Assassination of Julius Caesar* (2003), and *Democracy for the Few, 9th edition* (2010).